Basic Cognitive Processes

WITHDRAWN

Basic Cognitive Processes

Judith Greene
and
Carolyn Hicks

Open University Press

Milton Keynes

Open University Press
Celtic Court
22 Ballmoor
Buckingham
MK18 1XW
England

First published 1984
Reprinted 1989, 1991

British Library Cataloguing in Publication Data

Greene, Judith
    Basic cognitive processes
    1. Cognition
    I. Title   II. Hicks, Carolyn
    153   BF311

    ISBN 0-335-10582-3

Text design by W.A.P.

Cover design by Paul Clark

Phototypeset by Getset (BTS) Ltd, Eynsham, Oxford

Printed and bound in Great Britain at the Alden Press, Oxford

To Midge
To Peter

Contents

Preface

The aim of this *Open Guide to Psychology* is to provide revision materials for psychology courses in basic cognitive processes, covering the main topics of perception, attention, learning and memory, which form the backbone of most psychology syllabuses. This book contains the essential facts in summary form and provides a framework around which to organize revision, using the teaching techniques which have proved successful with Open University students, including diagnostic questions, key note summaries, indexes of concepts and methodology notes.

Who is this book for?

Perhaps it is important to stress that the *Open Guides to Psychology* are not designed to give training in the techniques needed to practise as an educational, clinical or industrial psychologist. What they do offer are specially designed revision programmes to ensure successful performance in the psychology courses which are necessary prerequisites for further specialised training.

For many training and research courses a degree in psychology is required, or alternatively a pass in the British Psychological Society's Qualifying Examination in Psychology. For other careers like teaching, social work, vocational guidance, speech therapy, nursing and counselling, to name just a few, courses in psychology form part of the syllabus. And there are increasing numbers of students taking 'A' level courses in psychology at school and college.

Whether studying psychology courses at 'A' level, degree level or as part of their professional training, students should find these revision guides helpful in their preparation for examinations.

We hope, too, that teachers of psychology courses will find this *Open Guide* useful for structuring the topic, presenting detailed information about techniques and providing many worked-through examples.

Introduction: How to use this guide

The aim of this book is to provide you with a guide to the essential information you will need in order to take an examination on the general topic of basic cognitive processes. Examination papers in this area go by many titles: 'cognitive psychology', 'cognitive processes', 'perception and attention', 'learning and memory', 'experimental psychology', 'general psychology' 'fundamental psychology' or 'fundamental psychological processes'.

It is in fact quite difficult to grasp just what is meant by 'cognitive processes'. Cognition is often defined as higher level mental processes going on inside our heads, such as conscious thoughts and feelings, making plans, having opinions and deciding what to say. But basic cognitive processes usually refer to the mechanisms underlying such activities as perceiving and recognizing objects, attending to sounds, learning simple responses and memorizing lists of items. These basic mechanisms are considered to be universal to all members of the human species, if not to the whole animal kingdom. The emphasis is less on the quality and individuality of each person's conscious thoughts; more on the physiological and psychological processes which cause humans to behave as they do.

The Four Modules

The book is organized into four modules to cover the main areas of 'Perception', 'Attention', 'Learning' and 'Memory'. As you will see when you come to study them, division into these separate topics is to some extent artificial; we as human beings do not see, attend, learn and memorize as separate activities but are continuously doing all at once. However, the modules do reflect separate psychological traditions, since research in the various areas started off with different conceptions of human behaviour and methods of investigation.

One of the biggest problems facing psychology students is how to set about trying to integrate all the different approaches into a coherent whole. It is in fact important to realize that researchers do start with different aims and assumptions. However, there are obvious interconnections and these have been indicated in the text by cross references between the four modules.

Historical Chart

To help you to compare the various approaches, the Historical Chart at the end of the book gives the dates of major psychologists and theories so that you can see how different lines of psychological research originated, developed and sometimes merged. There is also an Overview of Models on p.109 which shows how various formulations of basic cognitive processes relate to each other. Our advice is to refer to the Historical Chart as you are introduced to the research in each module. However, you should look at the Overview of Models only after you have studied all the modules.

Technique Boxes and Methodology Notes

Another source of confusion is the multiplicity of techniques and methods used in psychological research. To help you through the maze, each new technique for investigating behaviour is described in a Techniques Box.

The Methodology Notes explain the general basis for experimental methods in psychology and provide an overview of the methods used in each of the modules.

Index of Concepts and References

In order to help you find your way around the book, there is an Index of Concepts which lists all the concepts described in the text. The page numbers refer you back to where each concept was defined (shown in italics in the text).

There is also a list of References which gives the authors of books and articles, and a Names Index which lists the page numbers where they are referred to in the text.

Diagnostic Questions

Since this book is an 'Open Guide', it is essential that you should take an active part in assimilating the text rather than being a passive receiver of information. After all, you are the only person who can diagnose what you already know and what you need to learn. This guide will have been a complete failure if the information remains on the page rather than ending up inside your own mind!

Each module starts with General Diagnostic Questions. In each case, there is an indication of which section of the text is particularly helpful for answering each question although, of course, bringing in relevant information from other sections and modules would increase your grades. At the end of each module you will benefit from going back to the general diagnostic questions to see whether you now feel competent to tackle them.

Each section within a module starts with its own Diagnostic Questions. You should start by testing yourself to see whether you already have the required knowledge. The Key Notes at the end of each section summarize the essential points made in that section. You should make sure that you understand these summaries and the evidence on which they are based. Finally go back to the beginning of the section and pair up the Diagnostic Questions with the answers in the Key Notes.

Self Assessment Questions (SAQs)

It is equally essential that you attempt to answer every one of the Self Assessment Questions (SAQs) before you look up the answers at the back of the book. These SAQs are designed to test your understanding of theories and methodologies described in the text. Sometimes they require you to look back to other modules to point out similarities between superficially different theoretical approaches. It is foolish to go on reading without checking up that you really understand what is being said. You will only have yourself to blame if you ignore the SAQs, which have been devised solely for your own advantage.

Suggestions for Reading

Each module has a Reading Guide which suggests some general reading and specific reading for each section. References are made to Open University texts which contain further information about the various topics and other books are listed which you should find particularly helpful. Recommended books include two Open University courses: *DS262 Introduction to Psychology*, Units 3, 10 and 5-7, and *D303 Cognitive Psychology*, Units 6-7, 13-15; and 5, 12 (these are obtainable from the Open University Press, Milton Keynes). George Miller's *Psychology: the Science of Mental Life* provides an amusing and enlightening introduction to major psychological traditions, Lindsay and Norman's *Human Information Processing* is a classic in the area, and the recommended volumes in the Methuen *New Essential Psychology* series provide useful summaries.

How to progress through the book

1 (i)   Read and try to answer the General Diagnostic Questions for Module 1, the Perception Module.

(ii) Read and try to answer the Diagnostic Questions for Section 1.1.

(iii) Read Section 1.1 doing all SAQs.

(iv) Check Key Notes 1.1 against the Diagnostic Questions for Section 1.1.

(v) Proceed in the same way through Sections 1.1 to 1.8.

(vi) Look at Column 1 of the Historical Chart.

(vii) Read Sections 5.1 to 5.4 of Methodology Notes, including Methods for Studying Perception.

(viii) Go back over the General Diagnostic Questions for Perception to make sure you can answer them.

2   Go on to Module 2, the Attention Module, progressing through the sections in the same way and ending by looking at Column 2 of the Historical Chart and Sections 5.1 to 5.5 of Methodology Notes.

3   Go through Module 3, the Learning Module in the same way, ending by looking at Column 3 of the Historical Chart and Sections 5.1 to 5.6 of Methodology Notes.

4   Go through Module 4, the Memory Module in the same way, ending by looking at Column 4 of the Historical Chart, reading the whole of Methodology Notes, and studying the Overview of Models on p.109.

Final Revision

We would recommend you to go through the various components of this guide in the following order.

— First, check through the Index of Concepts to test whether you know what they all mean, looking up the definitions of any you are still unsure about.

— Next, look at the Historical Chart (and Overview of Models) to remind yourself of the general theoretical frameworks within which psychologists have studied basic cognitive processes. Look also at the Methodology Notes and refer back to any Techniques Boxes you need to revise.

— Now go through each module in turn, testing yourself on the Diagnostic Questions for each section, referring to the Key Notes to check your answers. If you don't understand the Key Note summaries, read through the section again, retesting yourself on the Self Assessment Questions.

— When you are happy with your knowledge of all four modules, try answering the General Diagnostic Questions for each module. These questions are very like the types of questions you will find in examination papers. It will be a real help in your preparation for the exam if you map out plans of how you would answer all these questions. Try writing at least some of them out in full as examination answers, taking about 45 minutes on each, since the most common exam format is four questions in three hours. You will find all the relevant information in the appropriate sections but remember that you can only improve your grades by bringing in relevant information from other sections and even other modules. The constant cross-references between the modules and the Historical Chart and Methodology Notes should give you some ideas about this.

Finally, good luck. Luck is undoubtedly a help in exams; but so also is confidence. We hope this guide will succeed in boosting not only your knowledge but also your confidence in psychology.

1

Perception Module

General Diagnostic Questions for Perception

1 Briefly describe the physiological sensory system underlying visual perception. (Section 1.1)
2 What can be learnt from psychophysiological studies? (Section 1.2)
3 Outline the Gestalt laws of perceptual organisation. (Section 1.3)
4 What is the relation between perceptual illusions and perceptual constancies? (Section 1.4)
5 What are the main differences between top-down and bottom-up processing? (Section 1.5)
6 Evaluate the evidence for perception being innate or learned. (Section 1.6)
7 Compare template, pandemonium and cyclic models of perception. (Section 1.7)
8 To what extent is perception affected by emotional states? (Section 1.8)

1.1 THE VISUAL SYSTEM

Diagnostic Questions for Section 1.1

1 Define the following: retina, optic nerve, visual cortex.
2 Describe how input is analysed by the visual perceptual system.

Human beings have five senses — sight, hearing, touch, taste and smell. *Perception* is the process by which the information from our senses is perceived by us. In this first module we shall pay most attention to seeing and hearing, since they are our principal senses. However, remember that we do have other senses which provide information for perception and that in some cases we recognize objects mainly through our secondary senses of taste and smell.

SAQ 1
What are the sense organs for each of the five senses? (Answers to SAQs p.110)

Within any sensory system there are a number of components. First there are nerve calls called *receptors* that are specialized for turning energy in the environment into electrical activity in the nervous system. In vision, the environmental energy is light which enters the eye through the pupil.

TECHNIQUES BOX A

Hubel and Wiesel's Studies

A fine recording needle (micro-electrode) is surgically inserted into the visual system of an anaesthetized cat and moved about until it is picking up the characteristic pattern of spontaneous electrical activity from a single nerve cell. Later when the cat is awake, it is placed facing a screen on which a small light is moved about. Changes in the activity of the single cell are recorded as the position of the light on the screen is plotted. This yields a visual 'map', known as a *receptive field*, for this particular cell (see Figure 1.1). Since a nerve cell will always show some spontaneous activity, the receptive field is that area in which the presence of a light changes (either increases or decreases) the spontaneous level of activity of that particular cell. This procedure is repeated to locate the receptive field of different cells. By changing the kind of input on the screen it is possible to compare the effects of different kinds of input: for example, a bar of light instead of a spot on the activity of each cell.

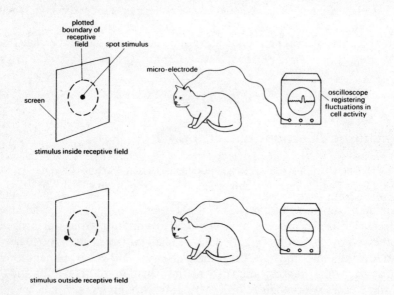

Figure 1.1   The recording technique used by Hubel and Wiesel

Recording from single cells at several levels of the visual system, from the retina up to the visual cortex, Hubel and Wiesel found that some cells are activated by different kinds of inputs in their receptive fields. Lower level cells respond to simple inputs like a stationary dot, a line or a moving dot. Cells higher up in the visual system are only activated by complex configurations, such as lines at specific orientations.

The visual receptors form a dense mosaic of nerve cells at the back of the eye comprising the *retina*.

Stimulation of the receptors causes *electro-chemical activity* which can be transmitted from one cell to another. Leading from the retina is the *optic nerve* which transmits nerve impulses to the part of the brain where primary analysis of visual sensations occurs, the *visual cortex*. In this way information about the environment from the receptors is transmitted to the appropriate brain cells. The problem of *perception* is to explain how input to the *sensory receptors*, known as *sensory information*, is transformed into what we actually see or hear.

Studying the activity of nerve cells at various stages in the *visual system* has shown that the analysis of input becomes more complex as information is transmitted upwards from the retina. A typical experiment of this type is described in Techniques Box A.

Hubel and Wiesel (1959) interpreted their results as demonstrating that visual input is analysed in a hierarchical manner, the nerve impulses from lower cells providing simple information which is organized into more complex combinations of lines, edges and moving dots which are passed up to cells higher up in the visual system.

Key Notes 1.1

1 At the back of the eye is the retina, a layer of nerve cells which act as receptors to receive light from the environment and convert it into electrochemical activity. This is transmitted along the optic nerve to the visual cortex in the brain.
2 Analysis of cell activity in the visual system has shown that information from cells in the retina is organized to transmit more complex information to higher cells in the visual cortex.

1.2 PSYCHOPHYSICS: THE STUDY OF SENSATIONS

Diagnostic Questions for Section 1.2

1 What is studied in psychophysics?
2 Briefly describe the methods used in psychophysics.
3 What are the main criticisms of psychophysics?

Psychophysics was developed in the first psychological laboratories in Germany at the end of the nineteenth century, notably by Wilhelm Wundt. These psychologists looked at perception from the point of view of people's actual experiences (rather than the working of the brain).

Psychophysics attempts to discover direct relationships between external physical inputs and subjective sensations of what we are aware of perceiving. They were interested in elementary sensations such as: (a) how soft can a sound get before we cease to hear it? (b) if the intensity of a light changes, how big must the change be in order for it to be noticed?

TECHNIQUES BOX B

Psychophysical Methods

In order to answer these questions thresholds have been studied. A sensory threshold is the minimum amount of stimulation needed for someone to report that they have experienced a sensation. A *threshold* is defined as the level of sound, light or touch at which someone reports hearing, seeing or feeling a sensation 50 per cent of the time. More recently, using sophisticated devices, Von Bekesy (1957) has shown that the ear is so sensitive to sound that, were it any more sensitive, we would begin to hear the actual air molecules as they bounce off the eardrum! In general, the study of thresholds has shown our senses to be highly efficient at turning environmental energy into perceptual sensations.

Psychophysical experiments were also carried out in which people were asked to report whether they noticed a change in input. For instance, sounds of two different loudnesses or pitches would be presented and people asked whether they could hear any difference between them. It was found that the amount of change in a sensory input that is just noticeable is a roughly constant fraction of the input. In a dark room lit by one candle the addition of a second candle is easily noticed. In a room lit by a hundred candles, adding a further candle would be undetectable. The amount of stimulation needed to produce a change in sensation is known as a *Just Noticeable Difference* (JND).

SAQ 2
Which would be detected more easily: an identical increase in noise level at a pop concert or a piano recital?

The psychophysicists believed that *elementary sensations*, which reflect simple aspects of our environment, like weight, colour, pitch and loudness, are the building blocks from which full perception of objects occurs. Indeed, one of the main objectives to psychophysics is that it attempted to study sensations in isolation rather than total perceptions. Loudness was loudness regardless of what object produced it; light was light regardless of its source.

Another criticism is that psychophysical investigations depend on people reporting the sensations they experience. This method of asking people to introspect about their own sensations, thoughts or feelings is known as the *introspective method*. Apart from the difficulty of checking whether these introspections are accurate, it turned out that people had to have a lot of practice before they could succeed in reporting isolated sensations, e.g. the brightness of a light or whether they could detect a touch on their skin. However, despite these criticisms of psychophysical methods, the methodology of carefully controlling inputs to see what effect small changes in stimulation have on reported perceptions has provided psychologists with a useful experimental technique for exploring people's perceptual abilities.

Key Notes 1.2

1 The study of elementary sensations is known as psychophysics.
2 Psychophysical methods involve asking people to report changes in input in order to establish thresholds of sensory stimulation and discrimination (JNDs).
3 Despite criticisms that the psychological approach implies that perception consists of isolated sensory elements, it has been influential in mapping the limits of the perceptual system.

1.3 GESTALT LAWS OF PERCEPTUAL ORGANIZATION

Diagnostic Questions for Section 1.3

1 Outline the fundamental principles of the Gestalt theory of perception.
2 List the laws of perceptual organization.
3 What was the Gestalt psychologists' explanation of the mechanisms underlying perception?

The German psychologists of the 1920s and 1930s, known as the Gestalt School, believed that psychologists should study the perception of whole figures (*gestalt* from the German word for shape or figure) rather than the elementary sense experiences that were the stock-in-trade of psychophysics. No study of individual sensory elements can add up to an adequate account of perceptual experience since 'the whole' (perception) is more than the sum of its 'parts' (sensations). Instead, the Gestalt psychologists wanted to discover what makes us see whole figures standing out against a background, known as the distinction between *figure and ground*. Wertheimer, a noted Gestalt psychologist, compiled a list of Gestalt *laws of perceptual organization*, four of which are illustrated in Techniques Box C. It should be pointed out that, despite their objections to the psychophysical approach, the Gestalt psychologists used the same

TECHNIQUES BOX C

Gestalt Laws of Organization

Proximity

Elements that are close together tend to be seen as forming part of the same figure against a background. In Figure 1.2(i) you can see either horizontal rows or vertical columns with equal ease. When some of the dots are closer together, either horizontal rows emerge (as in (ii)); or vertical columns (as in (iii)).

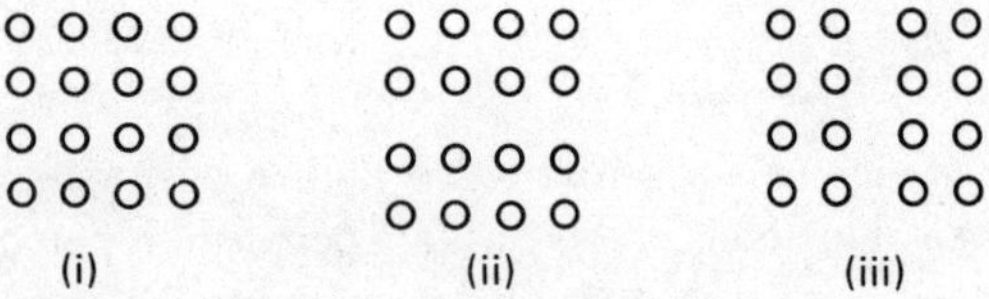

    o o o o   o o o o   o o o o
    o o o o   o o o o   o o o o
    o o o o   o o o o   o o o o
    o o o o   o o o o   o o o o
                     o o o o
       (i)   (ii)   (iii)

Figure 1.2

Similarity

Similar elements tend to be grouped together to appear as organized wholes; you tend to see columns rather than rows in Figure 1.3.

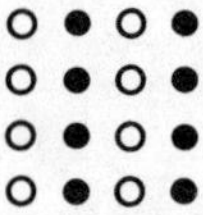

    o ● o ●
    o ● o ●
    o ● o ●
    o ● o ●

Figure 1.3

Closure

One of the best known Gestalt laws is the way in which incomplete lines are filled in to produce 'good' figures like squares or circles (see Figure 1.4).

Figure 1.4

Continuation

Figures tend to stand out against a background when they are defined by an uninterrupted contour (see Figure 1.5).

       (i)   (ii)

Figure 1.5

method of varying inputs and asking subjects to report their perceptual experiences.

SAQ 3
Looking at Figure 1.5, why is the number 4 more effectively concealed in (i) than in (ii), even though there are more irrelevant lines in (ii)?

The rationale given by the Gestalt School for the 'Laws of Organization' was based on their theory of how the brain works. They believed that the brain has certain innate electrical characteristics which organize sensory inputs according to the laws of organization. Thus an input of an incomplete figure is transformed by the perceptual system into a 'good' figure, so that is what we see. Gestalt psychology is often thought of as implying an active role for the perceiver in organizing perceptions as wholes. But their theory implied that perceptions are determined by a direct mapping of perceptual input into organized figures in the brain. Nevertheless, although their theory of brain mechanisms has proved to be wrong, their demonstrations of perceptual laws of organization still need explaining.

SAQ 4
Identify one way in which Gestalt psychology differs from psychophysics, and one way in which the two are similar.

Key Notes 1.3

1 The basic tenet of Gestalt psychology is that perceptions are organized into whole figures and ground.
2 Some Gestalt laws of organization are described in Techniques Box C.
3 Gestalt psychologists believed that perceptions are caused by activity of the brain which reflects the organization of sensory inputs into figures and ground.

1.4 PERCEPTUAL CONSTANCIES AND ILLUSIONS

Diagnostic Questions for Section 1.4

1 Define size constancy.
2 List some cues which determine the distance of an object.
3 What is a possible explanation for the Ponzo illusion?
4 Evaluate the evidence for cross-cultural differences in the way illusions are perceived.

From the earliest days of psychological research psychologists were aware of the phenomenon of *perceptual constancy*. This refers to the fact that we tend to see objects as the same (i.e. a constant) size and shape despite the fact that objects throw very different images on the retina, depending on their distance and orientation.

Figure 1.6 shows that the nearer an object (represented by an arrow), the larger the image on the retina. Although the arrow is the same size at further distances, the retinal image gets smaller. Yet objects are seen as roughly the same size regardless of the size of their retinal image. As people walk away they don't diminish into pygmies. This is what is meant by *size constancy*.

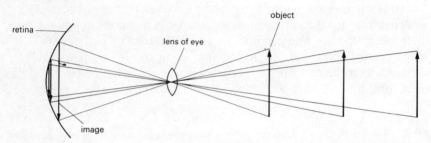

Figure 1.6 The relationship between object distance and retinal image size

The problem of size constancy is that the sensory information from receptors in the retina is providing 'false' information about the size of the object (i.e. a tiny image when the object is at a distance) and yet we perceive it as its normal size. In order for this to happen, the visual system must have some way of allowing for distance so that the image on the retina can be transformed into a perception which reflects the 'real' size of the object. This means that retinal receptors must pick up information about the distance of an object. The visual system would then be able to take account of the sensory information from the retinal receptors about both the size of the image on the retina and its distance, allowing it to compensate for the small image cast by a distant object, so that we as perceivers 'see' it as the correct size. Some possible visual cues to distance are shown in Figure 1.7.

SAQ 5
(a) which looks nearer, circle or square?
(b) which looks nearer, pencil or van?
(c) which looks nearer, square or triangle?

In these examples the visual system ends up with a 'true' perception of the real size of an object. However, psychologists have also been interested in *perceptual illusions*. These are cases when perceptual processes go

Figure 1.7 Distance cues in perception

wrong, the idea being that an understanding of the mechanisms involved may throw light on normal processing.

Most of the illusions which have been studied are visual illusions, examples of which are the Ponzo and Muller-Lyer illusions shown in Techniques Box D.

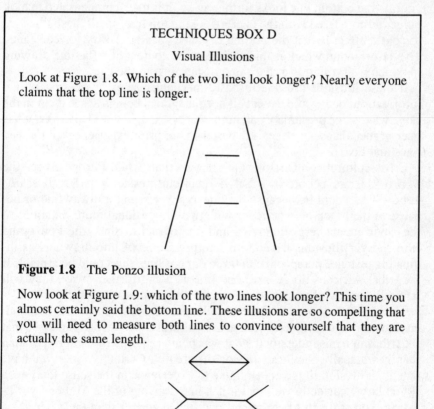

TECHNIQUES BOX D

Visual Illusions

Look at Figure 1.8. Which of the two lines look longer? Nearly everyone claims that the top line is longer.

Figure 1.8 The Ponzo illusion

Now look at Figure 1.9: which of the two lines look longer? This time you almost certainly said the bottom line. These illusions are so compelling that you will need to measure both lines to convince yourself that they are actually the same length.

Figure 1.9 The Muller-Lyer illusion

Gregory (1966) has proposed an explanation of these illusions in terms of overcompensation of basic size-constancy mechanisms. In the Ponzo illusion the perspective of the 'railway lines' makes it look as if the top line is further away. According to the laws of constancy, the size of the retinal image of this line is compensated for to allow for its distance, and so the line is perceived as looking bigger. However, since the illusion is a two-dimensional drawing, the lines are actually at an equal distance from our eyes; so the normal compensation for distance results in overcompensation of the size of the 'further away' top line, making it look bigger than it really is.

The Muller-Lyer is similarly explained by imagining that you are looking at the figures in 3D representations. In Figure 1.9 imagine that the bottom line looks as if it is the far side of a box facing towards you while the top line looks as if it might be the near edge of a box facing away from you. As the bottom line looks further away, it is over-compensated to look bigger as compared with the nearer-looking top line. In all these illusions the basic effect is that the normal distance cues necessary for constancy give information which is misleading in the context of a flat line drawing in which everything is at the same distance from the eye.

If these illusions are due to basic mechanisms for processing retinal information, one would expect all normal human beings to see them in the same way, since presumably all human eyes are the same. However, it has been argued that such effects are based on our prior experiences of railway lines and boxes.

Cross-cultural comparisons have shown that, while Europeans see the Ponzo illusion, people in tribal African cultures do not (Segall *et al.*, 1966). This could be because they have never seen a railway line or because of their lack of experience with two-dimensional representations of the environment, e.g. diagrams and photographs. Since the Ponzo and Muller-Lyer illusions depend on interpretations of line drawings as indicating distance perspective in three dimensions, this could be crucial. If the tribal Africans don't 'see' one line as being further away, they will naturally see two lines of equal length drawn on a piece of paper.

These results should be treated with some caution, since it is not at all easy to carry out completely fair cross-cultural experiments. It may be that the tribesmen misunderstood what was being required of them rather than that they actually 'saw' the illusion differently. Certainly, once you have 'seen' an illusion, it is very immune to experience in the sense that, even if you know perfectly well that it is a line drawing of the Muller-Lyer illusion, you still can't help seeing one line as longer than the other.

SAQ 6
Which of the cues to distance in Figure 1.7 is operating in the Ponzo illusion in Figure 1.8?

Key Notes 1.4

1 Size constancy is the ability to recognize the 'real' size of an object, taking into account distance and image size on the retina.
2 We gain information about distance from a variety of cues: interposition of one object in front of another, familiarity with the actual size of objects and perspective cues.
3 The Ponzo illusion is a classic example of an illusion which depends on the observer assuming that objects are at different distances, and so over-compensating for size, when in fact the two lines are part of a flat line drawing at the same distance from the eye.
4 It is claimed that the perception of illusions can be affected by cultural experiences, but it is difficult to assess whether this is due to real perceptual differences or to a misunderstanding of the task.

1.5 BOTTOM-UP AND TOP-DOWN PROCESSING

Diagnostic Questions for Section 1.5

1 What is meant by bottom-up processing?
2 What is meant by top-down processing?
3 Give examples of bottom-up retinal cues about the distance of objects in the environment?
4 Why is top-down processing necessary to explain some aspects of perception?

So far we have been talking about basic mechanisms for analysing information received by sensory receptors. This is known as *bottom-up processing* because it starts with the lowest level of sensory inputs to the retina and works upwards to higher levels of perceptual analysis, i.e. it works from the bottom up.

Gibson (1966, 1979) is a psychologist who has stressed the importance of retinal cues for determining what we see. Figure 1.10 shows how information relevant to perceiving the distance of objects can be provided by physical cues, such as textures and gradients, in the *visual field* which falls on the retina. As mobile creatures we are constantly receiving information from different points of view. Gibson believes that this provides us with sufficient bottom-up information to explain how we can perceive features of our environment.

This approach to perception has been described by Gibson as the *ecological approach*, to emphasize that information from the whole physical environment is available for analysis by the receptor cells in the retina.

This kind of analysis is also known as *data-driven processing*, because it is the information data provided on the retina which 'drives' perception.

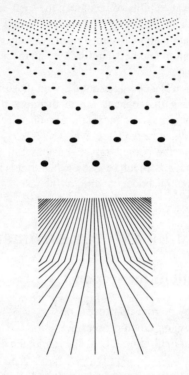

Figure 1.10

SAQ 7
Look back to Figure 1.7. Which of the cues to distance could be explained by bottom-up processing depending on sensory inputs to the retina?

As you have probably guessed, top-down processing is the reverse of bottom-up. The basic idea is that bottom-up sensory information from the retina is not enough to explain how we perceive objects and events; also relevant is the knowledge we already have about what things ought to look like. This is called *top-down processing* because expectations about the world and concepts of what objects look like are already stored in our heads, and work downwards to influence the way we interpret input received by our sense organs. Since it is concepts about what to expect in our environment which are involved in top-down processing, it is also referred to as *concept-driven processing*.

One of the main kinds of evidence for top-down processing is our ability to make sense of incomplete and ambiguous information. The point about ambiguous input is that an identical input on the retina can be interpreted (i.e. perceived) in more than one way. If the sensory inputs are the same, any differences in how we perceive the inputs must depend on our prior expectations about what is likely to occur in a particular context. Read the sentences in Figure 1.11. What is the first word in the first sentence and the third word in the second sentence? The perception of two different words depends on context, although the physical cues on the retina are exactly the same.

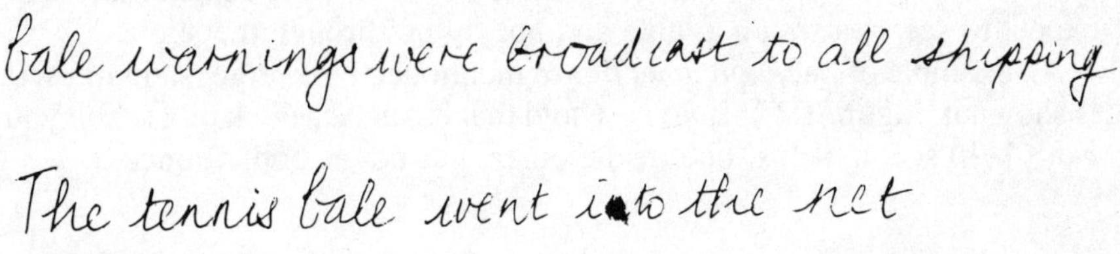

Bale warnings were broadcast to all shipping

The tennis bale went into the net

Figure 1.11

Read aloud the two sentences below. How do you 'hear' the italicized words, although the sensory inputs to your ears are the same?

If you tickle my feet *I scream*.
Would you like *ice-cream* or crisps?

What these examples show is that top-down processing allows us to make use of expectations based on past experience to make sense of what we see. The important point to grasp is that perception cannot be an exact copy of the input to the retina; otherwise how could an identical input be interpreted in two different ways? Something must be added from our own experience to explain these perceptions.

SAQ 8
Which of the cues to distance in Figure 1.7 in Section 1.4 is an example of top-down processing?

SAQ 9
Think of one example of pure top-down processing (i.e. when there is no retinal input).

Bottom-up and top-down processing have often tended to be thought of as rival explanations of perceptual processing. But, apart from slightly bizarre experiences like hallucinations, perception must always be a combination of both. We do not go around deciding what we are going to see in a purely top-down manner; nor do we observe brightness and other sensations in their pure bottom-up form. One problem is that perception is so instantaneous that we are unaware of all the processing going on in order to arrive at a final perception. We don't 'work out' that the top line of the Ponzo illusion looks further away; we simply see it as a longer line.

It is not surprising that we are not conscious of the physiological processing taking place in the cells in the retina and the rest of the visual system. But we are usually just as unaware of any *unconscious inferences* we are making to combine bottom-up sensory information and top-down knowledge in order to 'see' − for instance, in the way I see the familiar coffee mug on my desk as I am writing this. Wittgenstein, the famous philosopher, describes perception as 'seeing as', in the sense that we are constantly interpreting the evidence of our senses. It is only when we are faced with sensory information that we find hard to interpret that we might start to work out what something must be. For instance, we normally expect to see saucers on a table and not flying through the sky!

An example of an *ambiguous figure* mentioned by Wittgenstein himself is shown in Figure 1.12. If you are told that it can be a duck or a rabbit you can't help seeing it 'as' one or the other, but not as both at once.

Figure 1.12

SAQ 10
What is the relation between sensory inputs and perceptions for (a) ambiguous figures and (b) perceptual constancies?

Key Notes 1.5

1 Bottom-up processing works upwards from input to our sense receptors to higher perceptual analysis. This is also known as data-driven processing.
2 Top-down processing works downwards using knowledge of past experiences to interpret sensory input in terms of expectations about the environment. This is also known as concept-driven processing.
3 Gibson stresses the availability of texture and gradient cues about the distance of objects in the environment as reflected in the visual field on the retina.
4 Top-down processing based on knowledge and expectations is necessary to perceive sensory inputs 'as' familiar objects in our environment, a process which is demonstrated in our perceptions of ambiguous figures.

1.6 PERCEPTION: INNATE OR LEARNED?

Diagnostic Questions for Section 1.6

1 What is the relation between whether perception is innate or learned and whether it is bottom-up or top-down?
2 What is the evidence for perception being innate?
3 What is the evidence for perception being learned?

Obviously it is of vital importance for us to be able to judge the size, distance and orientation of objects as we move around. This applies even to very young children; so the question is, do we have to learn to see or are we born with perceptual abilities? Abilities that we are born with are called *innate* and these are contrasted with activities we have to learn. Learning will be defined more fully at the beginning of the Learning Module.

SAQ 11
Do you think that bottom-up processing is more or less likely to be innate than top-down processing?

Even if you accept that both bottom-up and top-down processing are involved in perception, it is an interesting question how much of even the basic visual mechanisms babies have available from birth. Experiments with young babies, some only a few days old, have shown that visual events like the sight of an object looming up are interpreted by very young babies as they would be by an adult (Bower, 1977), indicating that the baby sees the object as a constant size (size constancy) rather than as a series of isolated sensations. Babies have also been shown to react to human faces more than to other equivalent stimuli, as shown in Techniques Box E. If these observations are correct, they are strong evidence that we are born with the ability to interpret basic retinal events in terms of what they represent in the real world, i.e. as objects moving in our environment, and possibly as typically human objects.

Another way of establishing which aspects of perception are learned and which innate is to look at adults who have been blind since birth and whose sight is later restored. If they immediately perceive in the same way as someone sighted from birth, one can assume that perception does not have to be learnt. If they have to practise before being able to see properly, then it is probable that perception is a learned ability. While there have been a number of studies of this type, no clear-cut answer has emerged. One study of a man who had his sight restored at the age of 52 found that he could only identify objects subsequently by touch and not by looking at them (Gregory and Wallace, 1963). However, it has been argued that it might be his many years' dependence on other senses which was interfering with the use of vision.

TECHNIQUES BOX E

Fantz's Scrambled Faces Experiments

Experimenting with babies is difficult because they have no language to tell you what they are seeing. So it is necessary to find other ways of assessing what they are perceiving. Fantz (1961) made use of the fact that even very small babies fixate their eyes on things which interest them. Fantz showed *neonates* (newborn babies) different designs and measured how long the babies stared at them. He found that they spent most time looking at a drawing of a human face. This could not be explained as a preference for complex designs because a design including all the face features scrambled up did not attract their attention for such long periods (see Figure 1.13).

Figure 1.13
Source: Scientific American, W. H. Freeman.

The early work on elementary sensations, organization of figures and perceptual constancies described in Sections 1.1 to 1.4 assumed that perceptions are the result of innate mechanisms for processing sensory information. However, since the 1950s, there has been more appreciation of the role of learning from experience in perception as described in Section 1.5. In general, studies of both children and adults indicate that certain basic mechanisms, such as figure/ground and size constancy, are built into the physiological sensory system; if they were not, how would babies be able to learn anything from objects in their environment? On the other hand, recognizing complex objects and interpreting ambiguous cues depends on experience and learning.

Key Notes 1.6

1 It is usually assumed that bottom-up processing of retinal information depends on innate sensory mechanisms while top-down processing depends on learned experience.
2 The evidence from studies of infants demonstrates that at least the most basic mechanisms for perceiving moving objects are innate and that there is

possibly an inborn mechanism for recognizing human faces.

3 The evidence from adults with restored sight is equivocal but indicates that complex processes like recognizing objects may depend on appropriate experiences.

1.7 MODELS OF OBJECT RECOGNITION

Diagnostic Questions for Section 1.7

1 Outline one major problem of the template model of object recognition.
2 Describe feature detection models of object recognition.
3 How does the Pandemonium model work?
4 Describe Neisser's cyclic model of perception.
5 What does such a model imply about the perceiver?

The research described in previous sections was mainly concerned with different aspects of sensory information, such as the loudness of sounds, the lengths of lines, the size and distance of objects and the grouping of figures. In this section we will be describing models of *object recognition* which attempt to explain how all these separate sources of information are brought together so that people are able to recognize and identify objects. This is also known as *pattern recognition* because the problem is to explain how we are able to interpret patterns of sensory features as objects in our environment. You will notice that many of these models are concerned with recognizing letters and it is no coincidence that this is one of the primary tasks for computers. The rationale for a lot of recent research into perception is that, if you can work out what operations are necessary to feed into a computer to enable it to recognize objects, then you will understand a lot about what mechanisms must be involved in human vision. As you will see, it has not proved at all easy to work out how people are able to recognize even such simple objects as letters.

One of the simplest explanations of how we recognize objects is by *templates*. This idea is rather like that of a stencil in reverse, a detector in the visual system that is 'tuned' to recognizing a particular shape or pattern. When an input arrives which exactly matches a template, the template is activated (see Figure 1.14).

One problem is that there would have to be a template that exactly matches the input from every object we can recognize. The row of 'A's' in Figure 1.15 are just a few of the many styles of 'A's' that might be encountered. If the template theory is correct, we should have to have a separate template for every possible 'A' in order to recognize it!

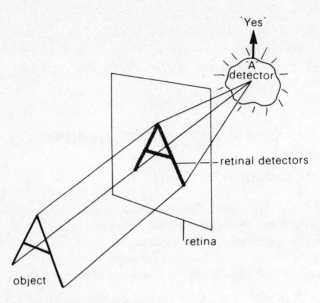

Figure 1.14   Template recognition

a A*a*A𝒂**a**𝒜

Figure 1.15

SAQ 12
Can you think of a set of letters which a computer system using a template for each letter
could cope with easily?

Obviously ordinary printed and written letters are more like those shown
in Figure 1.15, or in Figure 1.11 in Section 1.5 where exactly the same
squiggle is perceived as a 'G' in one sentence and a 'b' in the other. It was
the need to explain these facts that motivated an alternative explanation of
how we recognize objects. Instead of having to match whole templates
(like an 'A'), perhaps we recognize objects by detecting features like
lines, corners and curves. This is known as the *feature detection* model of
object recognition.

How might information from feature detectors be combined to allow us
to recognize patterns of features as objects? One suggestion is that feature
detectors are arranged in a hierarchy which starts by detecting simple
features and ends with the detection of complex patterns. One version of
this is known as the *Pandemonium model* (Selfridge, 1959). Selfridge
proposed a recognition system based on feature detectors called 'demons'

which 'shout' when they detect a particular feature. At any level, demons listen to the shouts of demons below them in the system and shout to demons above them in proportion to how much evidence they hear for their own particular pattern − the result is 'pandemonium' (see Figure 1.16). In this way information from lines is combined to produce angles and finally whole letters.

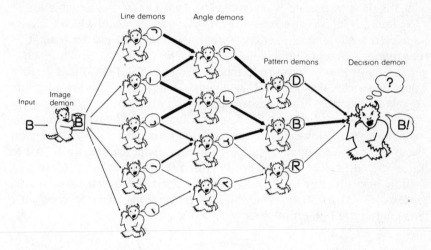

Figure 1.16   Pandemonium

The advantage of this system is that features can be assessed on a probabilistic rather than an all-or-none basis. When a feature is analysed at the first level it is compatible with several letters. A 'B' will be recognized as a 'B' if it has more features in common with a 'B' than any other letter, even if it is not a perfect example of a B. This seems to be a more plausible model of perception than the template one. One drawback of the Pandemonium model is that it does not take context into account; yet humans are obviously much more likely to decide that something is an O than a Q in the context C-T. This could be built in by including demons who shout for letters which are more likely to occur in a word or a sentence.

SAQ 13
Given a recognition system such as Pandemonium, which other letters would you expect to create most difficulty when looking for a Q? Which letters would make it an easy task?

SAQ 14
Which of the theories of perception described in Sections 1.1 and 1.3 might give support to template or feature detection models?

SAQ 15
Are templates and/or the Pandemonium model bottom-up or top-down models?

Both template and feature detection models start by analysing inputs. A different approach to object recognition is to assume that perceivers start with hypothetical perceptual models of the objects they are likely to encounter and use these models in a top-down direction to interpret inputs to their senses. But where do these hypothesized models of objects in the environment come from? People may have many different hypotheses which represent their expectations about objects but how do they know which is the appropriate perceptual model for any particular situation?

Neisser (1976) proposed an *analysis-by-synthesis* model which includes both feature extraction from the environment (analysis) and the generation (or synthesis) of perceptual models to guide the search for further features which might support the current model (see Figure 1.17). This is a *cyclic model* in which a first preliminary analysis of features (bottom-up) might suggest a perceptual model that an object is, say, a chair, leading to a (top-down) search for other expected features such as whether the object has a cushion or not. However, if the features from the environment start disconfirming the original hypothesis, then a new perceptual model has to be generated. An example might be when we realize that a mysterious shadow is really a heap of clothes over a chair. Each perceptual model represents a perception, although our perceptions may be constantly changing as we reinterpret what we are seeing.

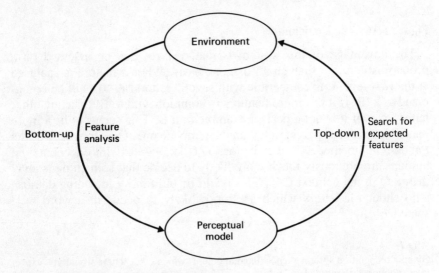

Figure 1.17 Neisser's cyclic model

Neisser makes the point that perception never occurs in 'a vacuum' but that our expectations and knowledge provide a mental model which directs our perceptual systems to hunt through the mass of sensations for evidence for expected objects and events. These perceptual mental models are also known as schemas; input cues are matched to a *schema* of an object or event which represents the expectations of the perceiver. Neisser's theory is an interactive model since he believes that perception results from a constant interaction between bottom-up feature analysis and top-down expectations.

SAQ 16
Suppose you are weeding in the garden. Which cyclic processes are likely to be involved in deciding whether a young plant is a flower or a weed?

You can see from examples like this that we have come a long way from investigating elementary sensations like changes in the loudness of a tone. The role of the perceiver is an active one, seeking out features and checking hypotheses, a very different picture from the passive role of even the 'head demon' in the pandemonium model. However, the notion of an active perceiver must not be taken as meaning that the perceiver makes any conscious decisions about perception, except perhaps in special cases like setting out to identify a peculiar object. Most perception relies on instantaneous unconscious inferences, as discussed in Section 1.5; in fact, it is the natural 'easiness' of normal perception that has made it so hard to investigate.

SAQ 17
Identify two uses of the word 'model' in the following statement: 'Neisser's cyclic model of perception states that perceivers generate perceptual models of objects?

SAQ 18
Which aspects of Neisser's model involve bottom-up processing and which top-down processing?

Key Notes 1.7

1 The template model of object recognition implies that there must be a separate template to match every object we can recognize.
2 Feature detection models assume that we have feature detection mechanisms for analysing individual features of objects such as lines and edges.
3 The pandemonium model is a hierarchical system for passing information from lower level detector mechanisms up to higher levels of analysis until final recognition of an object occurs.
4 According to Neisser's cyclic model of perception, perceivers generate perceptual models of objects which they use to interpret features and to initiate a search for further features to confirm their expectations.
5 In Neisser's model the perceiver is thought of as an active processor who integrates information from both bottom-up feature detection and top-down hypotheses based on prior experience, although this processing usually occurs at an unconscious level.

1.8 EMOTION AND PERCEPTION

Diagnostic Questions for Section 1.8

1 What is meant by perceptual defence?
2 What do perceptual defence experiments imply about perceptual processes?

As we have seen, perception is not just a bottom-up passive reception of external input but involves active top-down interpretations of inputs based on previous experience of objects in particular contexts. Such experiences will obviously include emotional experiences which may affect how certain objects and events are perceived. One type of study which attempts to tap the effects of emotional states on perception is described in Techniques Box F.

TECHNIQUES BOX F

Perceptual Defence Experiments

Bruner and Postman (1947) used a *tachistoscope* to study perceptual defence. This is a piece of apparatus commonly used in psychology which enables an input to be flashed on a screen for very short lengths of time, some of these exposures being so short (a few thousands of a second) that the viewer does not report seeing anything.

Bruner and Postman showed people four-letter words, some of which were neutral, and the rest of which were taboo 'four-letter' words. The initial exposures were very brief and people were requested to report each word. If they were unable to do so, then the exposure time was systematically increased until they could recognize it. Bruner and Postman found that people took significantly longer to report the obscene words than the neutral words.

Bruner and Postman argued that the taboo words aroused such emotional anxiety that people 'defended' themselves against seeing them, which is why they called it *perceptual defence*. In other words, even while the subjects were still unconscious of the words, i.e. could not see them, this still inhibited their conscious perception. This is also known as *subliminal perception* (*sub limen* means 'subthreshold') implying that, although the input is below the threshold of stimulation which can be reported, it still affects the length of time people take to make a response.

SAQ 19
Look back to the definition of threshold in Techniques Box B in Section 1.2. Why is the term subliminal perception appropriate for inputs which people are not aware of?

There are, however, two other possible explanations for these experimental results. One is that people did see the obscene words but simply didn't want to report them out loud in front of the experimenter. Another explanation is that people were so far from expecting taboo words in a psychological experiment that their top-down hypotheses were more likely to rule them out than facilitate perception.

These kinds of experiments raise crucial questions for all theories of perception. Whereas earlier work demonstrated that people can consciously detect sounds and lights, figures from ground, and are susceptible to perceptual illusions, it is much more difficult to investigate the unconscious processes that produce perceptions.

SAQ 20
What implications does this have for experiments which rely on people's introspective reports of their perceptual experiences?

Key Notes 1.8

1 Perceptual defence experiments investigate whether anxieties aroused by below-threshold inputs can affect conscious perception of words, although it is difficult to be sure that the emotion is affecting actual perceptions or only people's verbal reports of what they see.
2 Experiments like this emphasize the unconscious processes underlying perceptions, including the 'active' processes of generating and checking perceptual models.

READING GUIDE

General Reading

BARBER, P. J. and LEGGE, D. (1976), *Perception and Information*, London, Methuen.
BARBER, P. J. and LEGGE, D. (1985), *Information and Human Performance*, London, Methuen.
GREGORY, R. L. (1966), *Eye and Brain*, London, Weidenfeld and Nicolson.
MILLER, G. A. (1972), *Psychology: The Science of Mental Life*, Harmondsworth, Penguin, Chapters 7 and 10.
NEISSER, U. (1967), *Cognitive Psychology*, New York, Appleton-Century-Crofts.
OPEN UNIVERSITY *DS262 Introduction to Psychology*, Unit 5.
OPEN UNIVERSITY *D303 Cognitive Psychology*, Units 6−7.

Reading for each Section

Section 1.1: Gregory, Chapters 3, 4 and 5
            D303, Unit 6, Appendix 1
Section 1.2: Miller, Chapters 2 and 6
Section 1.3: Miller, Chapters 7 and 8
            D303, Unit 6, Section 2.2
            DS262, Unit 5, Section 3.1
Section 1.4: Gregory, Chapter 9
Section 1.5: *DS262*, Unit 5, Sections 2.3 and 6
Section 1.6: Gregory, Chapter 11
            DS262, Unit 5, Section 4
Section 1.7: *D303*, Unit 7, Sections 2 and 3
            Neisser, Chapters 3 and 4
Section 1.8: Neisser, Chapter 5

2

Attention Module

LINK FROM PERCEPTION TO ATTENTION

In the last module we often talked as though we perceive everything that happens in our environment. But if you think about it, that is impossible. Consider everything in your environment as you read this — everything in the room that you could see, hear, touch, smell and perhaps taste. Of course, you can become consciously aware of all these things if you pay attention to them. But that is just the point: do we attend simultaneously to everything in our environment or do we attend selectively to certain types of information at any one time?

The topics of perception and attention merge into each other since both are concerned with the question of what we become aware of in our environment. We can only perceive things we are attending to; we can only attend to things we perceive. Traditionally, however, these topics have been investigated in different ways. Investigations of perception have assumed that people are attending to the inputs they are presented with. Psychologists who have studied attention have concentrated on the factors that influence which inputs we attend to at any one time. Nevertheless, you will find that some of the same questions are at issue, notably the question of whether attention is governed by 'bottom up' sensory processes or 'top-down' expectations.

General Diagnostic Questions for Attention

1 What are the advantages of considering the brain as an information processing system? (Section 2.1)
2 What are the essential features of Broadbent's filter model? (Section 2.2)
3 Evaluate the evidence for Treisman's attenuation model of attention. (Section 2.3)
4 Distinguish between early selection and late selection models. (Section 2.4)
5 Assess the advantages and disadvantages of Kahneman's theory of attention. (Section 2.5)
6 What can we learn from dual task experiments about serial and parallel processing? (Section 2.6)

2.1 INFORMATION PROCESSING MODELS OF ATTENTION

Diagnostic Questions for Section 2.1

1 Outline a model of the brain as an information processing system.
2 Distinguish between input processes, storage processes and output processes.

For just a moment turn your attention to what you can hear going on around you as you are reading this text. If you are at home this may be the radio or TV, the tick of a clock, children playing outside, traffic. If you are on a train, it may be the conversations of other travellers, coughing, newspapers being rustled. You will probably become aware of many noises of which you were quite oblivious before.

The purpose of this activity is to demonstrate that, when we are selectively attending to one activity, we tend to ignore other stimulation, although our attention can be distracted by something else like the telephone ringing. Psychologists have been interested in what makes us attend to one thing rather than another, and why we sometimes switch our attention to something that was previously unattended.

One way of conceptualizing *attention* is to think of humans as information processors who can only process a limited amount of information at a time without becoming overloaded. Broadbent and others in the 1950s adopted a model of the brain as a limited capacity information processing system, through which external input is transmitted (as in a telephone system), and manipulated (as in a computer), with the output in the form of an active response (see Figure 2.1).

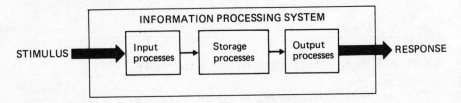

Figure 2.1 Information processing model of behaviour

In psychological models of this kind an input is called a *stimulus* because it stimulates the system (stimuli in the plural). All the perceptual inputs discussed in the 'Perception Module' are stimuli. In an information processing model stimulus input is thought of as information which is analysed and transformed as it is transmitted through the system.

Information processing models consist of a series of stages, or boxes, which represent stages of processing. Arrows indicate the flow of information from one stage to the next. In Figure 2.1, *input processes* are concerned with the analysis of stimuli. The next stage of *storage processes* covers everything that happens to stimuli internally in the brain, which can include coding and manipulation of stimuli. *Output processes* are responsible for preparing an appropriate response to a stimulus.

SAQ 21
Can you think of a common example of a system in which information is transmitted from input to output?

Attention theories are concerned with how information is selected from incoming stimuli for further processing in the system. Consequently they operate at the input processes end of the information processing model.

SAQ 22
At which stage of the model does perception occur?

Key Notes 2.1

1 A model of the brain as an information processing system assumes that external stimuli are transmitted through three major processes before a response is made.
2 Input processes are concerned with the analysis of stimulus information. Storage processes are concerned with storing and manipulating this information. Output processes are concerned with implementing appropriate responses.

2.2 BROADBENT'S FILTER MODEL OF SELECTIVE ATTENTION

Diagnostic Questions for Section 2.2

1 What is the cocktail party phenomenon?
2 Describe the split-span dichotic listening experimental procedure.
3 What conclusions can be drawn from Broadbent's experiments?
4 Discuss the implications of Grey and Wedderburn's results.

Donald Broadbent is recognized as one of the major contributors to the information processing approach, which started with his work with air traffic controllers during the war. Here we have a situation where a number of competing messages from departing and incoming aircraft are arriving continuously, all requiring attention. The air traffic controller finds he can deal effectively with only one message at a time and so has to decide which is the most important. In a quite different situation you may have had the experience at a party when there are a number of conversations going on around you. You can keep your attention on only one conversation despite all the noise, but you can often pick out bits of other conversations which interest you; for instance, if someone mentions your name. This is known as the *cocktail party phenomenon* (Cherry, 1953) — the use of the cocktail party analogy will alert you to the period in which this research was carried out!

The problem was how to design an experiment to investigate the processes involved in switching attention which are presumed to be going on internally inside our heads. To overcome this problem Broadbent used the dichotic listening technique described in Techniques Box G.

TECHNIQUES BOX G

Dichotic Listening: Broadbent's Split-Span Experiments

Dichotic listening means that inputs are presented through headphones attached to your ears, the point being that different inputs are presented to each ear. Broadbent (1954) developed an ingenious version of the dichotic listening procedure which he called the *split-span procedure*. People who take part in experiments are known as *subjects*. The subjects in Broadbent's experiment had to listen to digits through headphones; six digits were presented, three to each ear in simultaneous pairs, at half-second intervals (see Figure 2.2).

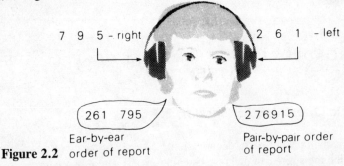

Figure 2.2   Ear-by-ear order of report   Pair-by-pair order of report

Subjects were then asked to recall the six digits in either of two ways:
(i) pair by pair, where they had to repeat the first pair of digits presented, followed by the second pair, then the third pair.
(ii) ear by ear, where they had to say the three digits from one ear, followed by the three digits from the other ear.

Broadbent found that ear-by-ear order of report was much easier for subjects and produced more accurate recall. This led Broadbent to suggest that the ears act like separate channels which can only be attended to one at a time. The pair by pair order of report requires continual switching between channels to retrieve each pair, one from the left ear and one from the right ear. This switching takes time and so reduces the efficiency of recall. Subjects find ear-by-ear order of report easier because it requires only one switch of attention from one 'ear' channel to the other. Since they can still successfully report some of the items presented to the other ear, these must be held in a temporary buffer store.

Broadbent (1958) proposed a *filter model* in which a *selective filter* selects one channel at a time. Information which does not pass through this selective filter is left in the sensory buffer store (see Figure 2.3).

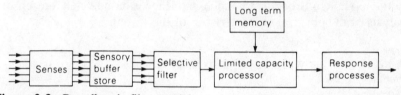

Figure 2.3 Broadbent's filter model

You may be wondering why this is a model of attention at all. The point of the limited capacity processor is that we can only deal with a few items at a time. This makes a filter necessary to confine our attention to input from a single channel so that we can deal with the items coming in on that channel one at a time. This concept of attention stimulated research into *selective attention*, so-called to emphasize the need to select which sensory inputs to attend to. The dichotic listening procedure became the most commonly used experimental method because it allowed experimenters to distinguish between attention to one ear or the other.

Broadbent's model has been termed a *single channel* theory of selective attention, since the perceptual processor can only process a single channel at a time. Moreover, the filter selects one channel on the basis of a sensory analysis of the physical features of the stimuli, like which ear they are coming from. Information from all other channels is stored very briefly in the sensory buffer store; this decays very quickly and after a second or two is completely lost.

In Broadbent's model the sensory buffer store and the selective filter form part of the 'input processes' which select which sensory inputs will be transmitted to the next stage in the information processing model. In fact, Broadbent's model can be thought of as a model of perception which tries to explain why only some aspects of the environment are selected at any one time for conscious perception. You should note that in this model attention precedes conscious perception since the filter operates at an early stage to select which sensory features will be passed through for further perceptual processing.

SAQ 23
Does this make Broadbent's model a top-down or a bottom-up model?

A number of studies have posed problems for Broadbent's model. Gray and Wedderburn (1960) demonstrated that it is not only physical features like the ear of arrival that determine channel selection. They gave their subjects items like 'cat seven mouse' in one ear and 'four ate eleven' in the other. Subjects found it easier to respond by switching ears so as to respond 'cat ate mouse' then 'four seven eleven' than by responding 'cat seven mouse' from one ear and 'four ate eleven' from the other. This experiment implies that some analysis of the meaning of the stimuli must have occurred prior to selection of channels; otherwise how could the categorization into numbers and meaningful words act as an aid for reporting the inputs? In Broadbent's model the filter is based solely on sensory analysis of the physical characteristics of the stimuli.

SAQ 24
What does Gray and Wedderburn's model imply about attention as a top-down or a bottom-up process?

Key Notes 2.2

1 The cocktail party phenomenon means that amidst a great deal of noise you are still able to attend selectively to one conversation.
2 In Broadbent's split-span dichotic listening procedure, six digits are presented, three to each ear in simultaneous pairs, and the subject is required to recall them pair by pair, or ear by ear.
3 The results from Broadbent's experiments suggest that the ears act as separate information channels. A selective filter operates on the basis of physical features to select a single channel to be processed at a time. The fact that two or three items from the other ear can subsequently be recalled points to the existence of a very temporary sensory buffer in which they can be held.
4 Gray and Wedderburn's experiment showed that non-physical features like the meanings of words can affect channel selection.

2.3 TREISMAN'S ATTENUATION MODEL OF ATTENTION

Diagnostic Questions for Section 2.3

1 What is Treisman's attenuation theory?
2 Describe the shadowing experimental procedure.
3 Identify one problem with dichotic listening as an experimental technique.

Accepting that people attend to only one channel at a time, Treisman set out to investigate what information, if any, can be processed even on an *unattended channel*. To do this, she used a technique called 'shadowing', developed by Cherry (1953), which is described in Technique Box H.

TECHNIQUES BOX H

Dichotic Listening: The Shadowing Procedure

Cherry's subjects heard tape-recorded passages of prose over headphones, two different texts being simultaneously presented one to one ear and one to the other ear. The task was to repeat out loud the passage coming in to one ear, a technique he called *shadowing* an attended message. The point about this task is that it is quite demanding to repeat back words you are listening to and so keeping up with the attended passage is likely to use up all your attention. Afterwards subjects were asked if they had noticed anything about the passage presented to the other unattended ear. Cherry found that they could report nothing about the content of the unattended text but they did notice if it was read by a man's or a woman's voice. Cherry's subjects seemed to have blocked out the non-shadowed message and were only aware of its general physical characteristics.

SAQ 25
Does this finding support Broadbent's theory or not?

Treisman (1960, 1964) extended this shadowing technique to investigate other differences between attended and unattended channels. In one experiment, Treisman used bilingual subjects. The attended message was in English and the unattended message was a French translation of the same story. The majority of subjects noticed that both messages had the same meaning. Clearly the content of the unattended message was not being ignored, suggesting that some meaningful analysis of the unattended message takes place. Another study by Treisman showed that, when the passage on the channel which is being shadowed is unpredictable in its sequence of words, switching to the unattended channel often occurs when there is a more likely word coming in on that channel.

As a result of these findings, Treisman suggested that the filter does not block out the unattended message completely, but only attenuates it; all information is passed on for further processing but only in a weakened form. Although only one channel is selected for further processing, the information from other channels is not lost altogether (see Figure 2.4).

In Treisman's model, information from *attenuated channels* can be passed on to the semantic analysis stage. *Semantic* is a term which means 'meaning' so Treisman thought of the recognition stage as the place where the meanings of input items are recognized. Even an attenuated input may be recognized if it is important to us and so we might hear our own name even though it occurs on an unattended channel.

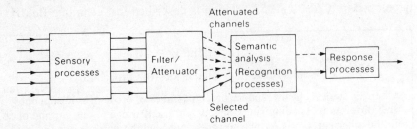

Figure 2.4   Triesman's attenuation model

SAQ 26
Suppose you were shadowing a text coming in on one ear and you heard 'there is a bomb in the room' in the other ear what would (a) Broadbent's and (b) Treisman's model predict in these circumstances? Would their predictions be different if you heard a fire-bell through the other ear?

The point to notice about Treisman's theory is that attention involves the recognition of meanings. Treisman's theory is equivalent to a model of perception in which one main channel is selected on the basis of sensory analysis for recognition, although inputs from attenuated channels have a chance of getting recognized as well. In other words, it is basically a single channel theory but with some allowance made for information from other channels.

There are, however, some problems with Treisman's theory. The nature of the attenuation process was never precisely specified. Recognizing the meaning of, say, a text in French requires a lot of analysis, but Treisman does not make it clear whether this amount of processing is possible for the attenuated messages on the unattended channel.

SAQ 27
Is Treisman's model top-down or bottom-up?

A final problem, which applies to all dichotic listening experiments, is that you can never be sure that the subjects may not have actually switched their attention to the so-called unattended channel. If they make rapid switches between the two channels, the ability to recognize aspects of the unattended message would not be the result of attenuated information from the unattended channel, since subjects would now be attending to the so-called unattended channel.

Key Notes 2.3

1 In Treisman's attenuation model the filter does not block out unattended channels completely but passes information on in an attenuated form.
2 The shadowing technique is a type of dichotic listening in which different messages are presented to each ear and the subject is asked to repeat aloud (i.e. 'shadow') one of the messages (the attended message); the message to the other ear is the unattended message.
3 The possibility that subjects are switching attention to items in the other ear rather than processing unattended information cannot be ruled out.

2.4 LATE SELECTION MODELS OF ATTENTION

Diagnostic Questions for Section 2.4

1 List some differences between 'early selection' and 'late selection' models of attention.
2 What was the principle idea behind the Deutsch/Norman model?
3 Evaluate evidence for late selection models.
4 What is the present status of perceptual filter models?

Broadbent and Treisman agree that selection of a single channel occurs at an early stage before recognition processes begin and so their models are called *early selection models*. An alternative view is that information from all channels is transmitted to the semantic analysis recognition stage and it is only after this that a selection is made. The general framework for a late selection theory of this kind was first proposed by Deutsch and Deutsch (1963) and was later elaborated by Norman (1968). Figure 2.5 shows a comparison between early and late selection models, indicating at which stage a selection is made from all the many sensory stimulus inputs.

The chief idea behind the Deutsch/Norman *late selection model* is that all stimuli gain access to the recognition stage of analysis. Items whose meanings are recognized as being most relevant and important are only then selected for further analysis. The fact that information from all channels is recognized before selective attention operates means that attention is not limited to a single channel but can select important inputs from any channel. Deutsch and Norman argue that the recognition process is not a bottleneck (i.e. it does not have limited capacity as in Broadbent's model) but nevertheless acts as a filter. It weighs each stimulus input against its relevance in the context of previous inputs, and passes on only the most relevant items into conscious awareness. The implication is that the prior recognition of the meanings of the inputs is an unconscious process.

Early selection model

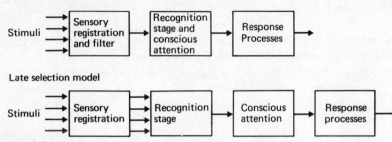

Late selection model

Figure 2.5   Early and late selection models

It may seem very bizarre to suggest that recognition and identification of an item can occur even before a person becomes consciously aware of what they have seen. You will remember that this issue of conscious awareness was raised in connection with the experiments on perceptual defence in Section 1.8 of the Perception Module, where it was assumed that people must have unconsciously recognized that a stimulus was threatening in order to prevent themselves from consciously 'seeing' it. The implication of this late selection model is that it is perception (i.e. recognition) which is unconscious and occurs before selection for conscious attention. In Broadbent's and Treisman's models selective attention occurs before conscious perception (i.e. recognition) of the meanings of items.

SAQ 28
How would the Deutsch/Norman model account for the fact that people are aware of some aspects of the content of an unattended message, like one's own name?

It is just this issue of conscious awareness that makes it difficult to test theories of attention. In Broadbent's and Treisman's models it can be presumed that people are only consciously aware after items have been selected by the filter; in Treisman's case with the possibility that some attenuated information may also attract conscious attention.

Deutsch and Norman explicitly argue that it is only after stimuli have been recognized and some have been selected for further analysis that they are consciously attended to. So, for both early and late selection models, selection occurs before consciousness. The point at issue is whether recognizing the meaning of stimuli is a post-selection stage (as in Treisman's model) or a pre-selection stage (as in the Deutsch/Norman model).

It was in order to test the Deutsch/Norman hypothesis of unconscious recognition of word meanings that experiments were designed to investigate whether the meanings of words in unattended messages can be shown to have an unconscious effect on subjects' responses to the attended message, even though they are not consciously aware of hearing anything on the unattended channel (see Techniques Box I).

TECHNIQUES BOX I

Effects of Unattended Messages

McKay (1973) required subjects to shadow ambiguous sentences such as 'they threw stones towards the bank yesterday' while either the word 'river' or 'money' was presented to the unattended ear. When subjects were after-wards asked which of two sentences was closer in meaning to the shadowed sentence, they selected sentences which contained interpretations of the ambiguous word 'bank' which were in agreement with the word presented in the unattended channel (e.g. They threw stones towards the side of the river); although they were not able to report which words they had heard on the unattended ear. This study lends support to the view that unattended material, although not consciously perceived, is undergoing a level of meaningful semantic analysis that can influence subjects' responses.

While studies of this kind are certainly compatible with a late selection theory, Treisman's theory could also account for these findings by saying that words like 'river' or 'money' were available in a weakened form from the unattended ear and so could facilitate the appropriate meanings for the ambiguous word 'bank'. Even Broadbent's theory could presumably say that the words 'money' or 'bank' were being held in the sensory buffer and so could be processed after the main channel and influence the final response.

SAQ 29
What happens to items on the unattended channel in Broadbent's, Treisman's and the Deutsch/Norman models?

The main difference between early and late selection theories is that early models assume that attention is based on a low-level sensory bottom-up analysis of physical features, such as ear of input, or the loudness of a message, which automatically attracts our attention. Late selection models allow for the fact that top-down analysis of the meaning of inputs can affect what we attend to. Both types of model, however, assume that all this processing goes on unconsciously before we become consciously aware of an input. In this sense attention can be equated with perception since, as far as attender/perceivers are concerned, the first thing they become aware of is recognition of the input. Moreover, both early and late models assume that only one set of items is finally selected for passing on to the processes responsible for generating a response. In McKay's experiment, for instance, only one interpretation of the sentence was responded to. Moreover, despite all the references in the models to selecting from a variety of input channels, the experiments themselves only looked at attention shifts between messages presented to one ear or the other.

In general, the difficulty of demonstrating at exactly what stage conscious attention occurs, resulted in psychologists shifting their own attention from the notion of restricting input to the question of how a limited attentional capacity can be allocated to cope with all the response demands made on it.

Key Notes 2.4

1 Late selection theories of attention assume that all incoming stimuli are passed on for recognition of their meanings prior to some items being selected for further processing. This is in contrast to early selection models which suggest that initial selection occurs at an earlier sensory stage in the perceptual process.
2 The Deutsch/Norman model is a late selection model which proposes that all stimuli gain access to the recognition stage and that it is only after their meanings have been (unconsciously) recognized that certain items are selected for conscious attention.
3 Evidence from shadowing experiments suggests that, even though unattended messages may not be consciously perceived, their meanings can affect responses made to attended inputs. However, results like these are also compatible with Treisman's attenuation model.
4 Psychologists have shifted their interest from bottom-up sensory filters to the question of how attention is allocated to deal with both inputs and responses.

2.5 KAHNEMAN'S CAPACITY THEORY OF ATTENTION

Diagnostic Questions for Section 2.5

1 How does Kahneman's theory differ from traditional models of attention?
2 Cite some evidence which supports Kahneman's model.
3 Outline one conceptual problem with Kahneman's theory.

Kahneman (1973) took up the notion that there is a certain amount of *attentional capacity* available which has to be allocated among the various demands made on it. On the capacity side, when someone is aroused and alert, they have more attentional resources available than when they are lethargic. On the demand side, the attention demanded by a particular activity is defined in terms of *mental effort*; the more skilled an individual the less mental effort is required, and so less attention needs to be allocated to that activity. If a person is both motivated (which increases attentional capacity) and skilled (which decreases the amount of attention needed), he or she will have some attentional capacity left over.

It follows from all this that people can attend to more than one thing at a time as long as the total mental effort required does not exceed the total capacity available. In Kahneman's model allocation of attentional resources depends on a *central allocation policy* for dividing available attention between competing demands (see Figure 2.6).

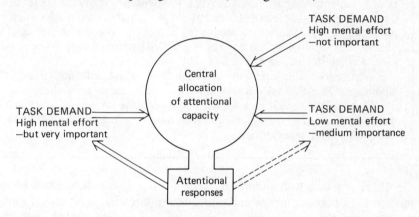

Figure 2.6 Kahneman's capacity model of attention

The picture that emerges from Kahneman's model is of attention as a central dynamic process rather than the result of an automatic filtering of perceptual input. The focus of interest is the way that the central allocation policy is operated so as to share appropriate amounts of attention between skilled automatic tasks and more difficult tasks which require a lot of mental effort. Another important aspect of Kahneman's model is that it looks at attention as a process which integrates perceptual analysis with the responses necessary to perform tasks. Rather than envisaging a one-way flow of information from input through to responses, attention involves a constant perceptual evaluation of the demands required to produce appropriate responses.

SAQ 30
Does Kahneman's model involve bottom-up or top-down processing?

Evidence for a model of this kind comes from *dual task experiments* which require people to do more than one task at a time, as described in Techniques Box J.

TECHNIQUES BOX J

Dual Task Experiments

The basic procedure is to give people two tasks to do at the same time, known as *concurrent tasks*. There are obvious difficulties in combining some activities, e.g. verbally shadowing two messages at once or singing and whistling at the same time. However, there have also been some striking experiments carried out by Allport, Attonis and Reynolds (1972) in which a pianist was able to sight-read music just as well as usual even when his attention was directed to shadowing a message coming in one ear. Shaffer (1975) demonstrated that a highly skilled typist could copy-type just as well when shadowing as when not.

Experiments of this kind imply that some well-learnt skills are virtually automatic. Once a decision has been made to drive somewhere, the actual driving of the car goes into 'autopilot'. And yet some form of unconscious monitoring of environmental requirements must be going on to enable us to deal with sudden emergencies.

One difficulty with Kahneman's model is the question of how much of the monitoring of task demands and allocation of attention is an unconscious process. On the whole we go about the business of coping with the ordinary demands of driving a car or cooking an egg while listening to the radio pretty automatically; and yet, when needed, we can also make a deliberate decision to give our full attention to a difficult task. So how are such decisions made about what to attend to? One easy way out is to assume that there is some operator who sits inside the allocation system deciding on policy strategies for allocating resources. The need for a 'little man' — known as a *homunculus* — to make decisions is often thought to be a weakness of a psychological theory, since the next question which could be asked is to explain what makes the homunculus make decisions: another little man inside him, and so on and so on.

Key Notes 2.5

1 Kahneman's theory differs from earlier theories in its emphasis on the active allocation of available attentional capacity between the attentional demands of competing responses. Rather than a one-way flow of information through a series of processing stages, it envisages a central allocation policy which monitors the resources needed for competing tasks.

2 Evidence from dual task experiments shows that people are able to do several tasks simultaneously as long as they are sufficiently skilled, so that the tasks do not demand too much attentional effort.

3 One problem with Kahneman's theory is that it does not explain how the allocation system decides on policies for allocating attentional recourses to tasks.

2.6 SERIAL AND PARALLEL PROCESSING

Diagnostic Questions for Section 2.6

1 Distinguish between serial and parallel processing.
2 At what point does parallel processing get converted into serial processing?
3 Explain the relationship between pre-attentional unconscious processes and conscious focal attention in Neisser's theory.
4 What is the distinction between central processor and multi-processor theories of attention?

As explained in Section 2.5, results from dual task experiments support the idea that people are capable of attending to several activities at once. This is known as *parallel processing* because it assumes that several processes are all taking place at the same time, i.e. in parallel. The original information processing model shown in Figure 2.1 in Section 2.1 of this module implies that each stimulus input is dealt with before the next stimulus input. This is called *serial processing* since each item is dealt with in serial order, one by one. This distinction is also known as *multi-channel* (parallel) *processing* versus *single channel* (serial) *processing*.

The Broadbent, Treisman and Deutsch/Norman models assume that conscious attention is serial in the sense that conscious attention is focused on selected inputs which are attended to one at a time. The question at issue between these models is at what stage inputs are selected as the focus of serial attention.

SAQ 31
Look back at Figures 2.3, 2.4 and 2.5 in Sections 2.2, 2.3 and 2.4. At what point do each of these attention theories suggest that parallel processing is converted into serial processing?

Of course, as we pointed out in Section 2.3, it is actually very difficult to decide whether people are switching very quickly between tasks or are genuinely processing more than one thing exactly at the same time in parallel. Neisser (1963) used a *visual search* task to investigate whether parallel processing is taking place (see Techniques Box K).

TECHNIQUES BOX K

Visual Search Technique

Neisser (1963) designed a visual search task in which subjects had to scan rapidly through a list of items to find a specified target item e.g. looking through a page of random letters to find a single target letter, say, an E.

BNKPM
CXHTW
HPTQS
XYYZK
JLRCS
HFMPT
SZKPF
RDSPN
HPVDC
DXNOG
RTGFN
LNFGY

Put your hand over the list of letters and then quickly take it away and start searching for an O. Now put your hand over the list again and this time start searching for any of the target letters A, E, I, O, U. You probably experienced two effects described by Neisser. One is that you glanced very rapidly at the letters until you came across the required target. Secondly, you almost certainly found the multiple targets much harder; although, if you noticed that they were the five vowels, you should have found it easier to reject the other letters as consonants.

Neisser's methodology was to record the *reaction times* subjects took between starting the search and locating a target. Despite the longer times initially taken to search for several targets at once, Neisser, Norick and Lazar (1963) found that after a great deal of practice searching for ten targets was only slightly slower and less accurate than searching for one target.

From these results Neisser (1967) developed a theory in which he distinguished between parallel processing of the background letters followed by a focusing of attention when a target is found and reported. Neisser believed that initial parallel processing involves an unconscious type of processing which he called *pre-attentional processes*, i.e. occurring before (pre) attention. *Focal attention* involves a conscious focusing of attention on the target item. Neisser's theory is not very different from the Deutsch/Norman model, since both allow for unconscious processing in parallel of all inputs up to the stage of conscious serial attention to single items. The initial parallel processing of letters in Neisser's task must involve unconscious recognition since the subject is able to reject those letters as not being the target item.

SAQ 32
This Neisser, is, of course, the same Neisser who developed the cyclic model described in Section 1.7 of the Perception Module. Look back to that model; what have Neisser's theories of perception and attention in common?

A final point about the parallel processing of two or more tasks is whether there is indeed a central amount of attentional capacity available, as in Kahneman's theory (Section 2.5), or whether we have separate processors for different types of tasks. In cases when people do two things at once, it is usual for the tasks to employ different *perceptual modalities*; for example, sight-reading music involves sight and hands while shadowing a message involves hearing and speech. When the typist in Shaffer's (1975) experiment was asked to type from an audiotape at the same time as shadowing a text in the other ear, she found this very difficult because both tasks involved listening. It is interesting to note that the dichotic listening task requires subjects to do just this, i.e. to attend to two auditory inputs at the same time, which might explain why early selective attention models concentrated on the need to select a single input channel.

Supporters of *separate processor theories* like Allport (1980) believe that separate processing systems can be called into operation without affecting the capacity of other modality systems, at least when people are skilled at performing tasks. This would mean that people are capable of parallel multi-channel processing as long as the tasks themselves involve separate channels.

This issue between serial and parallel processing is still an unresolved question. Nevertheless, common experience seems to bear out that it is possible to share one's attention between talking and walking, reading and listening to music, or at least to shift rapidly between them. On the other hand, the central processor can get so involved in one task that all other input recedes into the background; although 'attenuated' items may suddenly attract conscious attention if they become urgent, for example, the cry of a child or the door bell.

Perhaps the lesson that can be drawn from all this is that attention is a complex characteristic of human behaviour. All the models described in this Attention Module deal with partial aspects of attention; each can be shown to account for some of the evidence but not all. It seems likely that we do have a perceptual filter which cuts out information from irrelevant channels but that this can be overriden by meaningful analysis of inputs; that we are sometimes conscious of unattended information, like the rain outside a window or traffic conditions, but at other times monitor them at a pre-attentive unconscious level; that we are capable of attending to tasks using different modalities in parallel but that the central processor at times allocates all our attentional resources to a particular task. One crucial point is how skilled we are at tasks. The minimum attention needed for a well-learned task is quite different from the concentrated attention needed to learn new skills.

Key Notes 2.6

1 Serial (single channel) processing means that one input is dealt with at a time. Parallel (multi-channel) processing means that several inputs are processed simultaneously. The ability to perform two or more tasks at once has been interpreted as support for parallel processing, although it is difficult to rule out the possibility of rapid switching from one task to another.
2 A point at issue in attention models is at what point the flood of inputs impinging in parallel on our senses is selected for serial conscious attention. Early selection theories propose that this is done early in the perceptual process; late selection theories that an unconscious analysis of meaning takes place before a selection is made.
3 Neisser's theory of attention is an example of a late selection theory since pre-attentional processing includes the unconscious recognition of inputs before conscious focal attention.
4 Central capacity theories like Kahneman's assume that there is a central fund of attentional capacity which can be allocated to various tasks. Separate processor theories propose separate attentional systems for different modalities, allowing the possibility of multi-channel processing.

READING GUIDE

General Reading

BARBER, P. J. and LEGGE, D. (1985), *Information and Human Performance*, London, Methuen.
LEGGE, D. and BARBER, P.J. (1976), *Information and Skill*, London, Methuen.
NORMAN, D.A. (1976), *Memory and Attention* (2nd edition), Chichester, Wiley.
OPEN UNIVERSITY *DS262 Introduction to Psychology*, Units 6−7.

Reading for each Section

Section 2.1: *DS262*, Units 6−7, Sections 1.1, 1.2
Section 2.2: *DS262*, Units 6−7, Sections 1.4, 1.5, 1.6, 2.1
Section 2.3: *DS262*, Units 6−7, Section 2.2
Section 2.4: *DS262*, Units 6−7, Sections 2.3, 2.4
Section 2.5: *DS262*, Units 6−7, Section 5
Section 2.6: *DS262*, Units 6−7, Sections 2.5, 4.
         Legge and Barber, Chapter 7.

3

Learning Module

LINK FROM ATTENTION TO LEARNING

Both the Perception and the Attention modules have emphasized the importance of knowledge in determining what we perceive and attend to. But how did we acquire this knowledge in the first place? The obvious answer is through experience, including both formal school education and our general experiences of the world. Learning theories are concerned with how we learn from experience so that we can produce appropriate responses to deal with the environment.

Clearly, everything we learn must have been input in the first place. Psychological theories of learning have, however, tended to take input processes for granted. Moreover, the classical learning theories we shall be discussing in this module are often less interested in the storage processes stage of the information processing model than in the output of a learned response. In fact, they are sometimes called 'Black Box' models because they conceive of the mind as an empty black box. All they are interested in is the input (stimulus) which goes into the black box and the output (response) which comes out at the other end.

General Diagnostic Questions for Learning

1 List the basic propositions of behaviourism and their application to learning. (Section 3.1)
2 Describe the classical conditioning procedure. (Section 3.2)
3 What is the relation between response and reinforcement in operant conditioning? (Section 3.3)
4 Outline three main differences between classical and operant conditioning. (Section 3.4)
5 Why are punishments less effective than rewards? (Section 3.5)
6 Explain the relation between partial reinforcement and extinction. (Section 3.6)
7 Discuss two theories of secondary reinforcement. (Section 3.7)
8 What was Tolman's contribution to psychology? (Section 3.8)

3.1 LEARNING AND BEHAVIOURISM

Diagnostic Questions for Section 3.1

1 Which of the following changes in behaviour do you consider are instances of learning?
    (a) Adjusting your walk to the motion of a ship on a sea trip.
    (b) Mastering the contents of this unit.
    (c) Acquiring the ability to walk (as a child).
    (d) Walking unsteadily back from the pub.
2 What is behaviourism and why did it emerge?
3 Define S-R psychology.
4 What is the justification for using animals in experiments?

One very general definition of learning is anything which changes our behaviour. Starting with a newborn infant, one could say that learning is involved in everything which changes that baby into an adult equipped with the skills and knowledge necessary to deal with the world. Psychologists, however, have usually limited their definitions of *learning* to include only changes which are enduring, rather than temporary, and due to psychological factors, rather than physiological changes.

Learning is often contrasted with activities which are due to innate mechanisms. In the Perception Module, Section 1.6, there was some discussion about whether perception is the result of inbuilt physiological mechanisms or whether we have to learn to see. The implication was that babies are either born with the ability to see or not. But what about things like smiling? A baby may only start smiling after a few weeks and yet it seems odd to think of this as learning. People only develop their full height in their teens and yet we think of height as largely due to genetic heredity. Behaviour which is due to innate mechanisms but only develops at a later stage is known as *maturation*. As you can imagine, it is not always easy to disentangle what is due to maturation and what to learning. Intelligence is a noted example of an ability that seems to be the result of an interaction between innate potentialities and learning opportunities.

SAQ 33
Look back to Diagnostic Question 1 for this Section and, in the light of the above definition, decide which of the changes in behaviour listed there are examples of learning.

One thing you should note is the emphasis so far on behaviour as a measure of learning. Another way of looking at learning is to define it as increasing the knowledge in your head, the acquisition of skills and strategies for solving problems, all of which emphasize your potential for doing many things rather than learning specific behaviour.

The reason for the emphasis on behaviour in 'classic' theories of learning arose largely for historical reasons. In the early 1900s behaviourism developed as a reaction against theories based on *introspections*, i.e. people's verbal reports of their feelings and perceptions (see Section 1.2 of the Perception Module). J. B. Watson, the founder of behaviourism said 'Behaviourism . . . holds that the subject matter of psychology is the behaviour of the human being' (Watson, 1924). By this he meant the objective study of behavioural responses which could be measured, as opposed to 'unreliable' introspections.

Before describing in detail some of the basic tenets of behaviourism, some definitions may be useful. The term *organism* applies to any live animal, human or otherwise. A *stimulus* is any input or situation which can be described objectively. A *response* is any activity which can be observed and recorded.

Behaviourists generally assume that all behaviour is a response to a stimulus and hence it is often called *stimulus-response (S-R)* psychology. According to this view, learning is defined as a change in the response made to a particular stimulus as a result of an organism's past learning experiences. This led behaviourists to design experiments in which stimuli are carefully controlled and responses carefully measured to indicate that learning has taken place.

One consequence of this approach is that behaviourists, starting with Watson, declared that internal mental processes are quite irrelevant to explanations of behaviour. Their model of learning in effect collapses the information processing model shown in Section 2.1 of the Attention Module into the empty 'Black Box' shown in Figure 3.1. According to the classical behaviourists, the only proper topic for psychological study is the circumstances in which observable stimuli (S) get linked to overt responses (R). You should note the dates here though. If you look at the Historical Chart on p. 108, you will see that classical learning theories predate by many decades the information processing model developed in the 1950s. It would be a fairer description of events to say that later models opened out the 'Black Box' and started to fill up the mind with lots of little boxes representing stages of processing.

Behaviourists typically study animal behaviour. Accepting the implication of Darwin's theory of evolution that there is no sharp division between other animals and mankind, the behaviourists took advantage of the fact that animals are less complex and easier to study. A further advantage of using animals as subjects in experiments is that, since animals can't 'talk', there is no danger of relying on anything else than their observable behaviour. Behaviourists showed consistent results from their experiments at a time when introspectionists were floundering in controversies over whose introspections were correct. The result was a rapid growth in research from a behaviourist standpoint and a rapid decline in introspective studies.

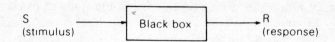

Figure 3.1 A simple black box

Key Notes 3.1

1 Learning is defined as a relatively enduring change in behaviour due to psychological factors, as opposed to innate, physiological and maturational factors.
2 Behaviourism is the objective study of the behaviour of organisms. It emerged as a reaction to the use of introspective methods in psychology.
3 In classic behaviourism, learning is considered to be the result of links between stimuli and responses (S-R).
4 Animals are used in experiments because they are less complicated and easier to control, the assumption being that anything discovered about how animals learn will be applicable to human learning as well.

3.2 CLASSICAL CONDITIONING

Diagnostic Questions for Section 3.2

1 What are the basic components of classical conditioning?
2 Why does classical conditioning occur?
3 Define extinction.
4 What is the difference between generalization and discrimination?

Classical conditioning is a type of S-R learning originally demonstrated in the late 1890s by Pavlov, a famous Russian physiologist (see Techniques Box L).

TECHNIQUES BOX L

Classical Conditioning

A dog stands in a soundproofed room immobilized by a leather harness. A bell rings, the dog turns towards it but otherwise shows little reaction. Five seconds later, food powder is presented to the dog through a long rubber tube. Ten minutes later, the bell again sounds and is again followed by food. The bell sounds for a third time but now the dog begins to move restlessly in his harness, saliva dripping from its mouth. As the trials continue, the dog becomes increasingly excited at the sound of the bell, more and more saliva flowing into a surgically implanted tube in its mouth, from which technicians can record the number of drops.

The concept of a *reflex* is an essential one in the study of classical conditioning. Miller (1972) defines it as:

> an involuntary, unlearned predictable response to a given stimulus (or class of stimuli), a response that is not influenced by any conscious thought or resolution but that can usually be seen to have some clear purpose in protecting the organism or helping it to adjust to the environment.

SAQ 34
List at least three human reflexes.

In the experiment described in Techniques Box L salivation is an innate reflex to the stimulus of food in the mouth and is therefore known as an *unconditional response* (UCR) to the *unconditional stimulus* of food in the mouth (UCS). To condition a reflex, there must also be present a *neutral stimulus* (NS), such as a bell, which does not elicit the innate response of salivation prior to the experiment. This neutral stimulus is presented to the organism (dog) together with, or just before, the unconditional stimulus (food), often enough for an association to be built up between them. This conjunction in time is crucial to conditioning and is known as the principle of *temporal contiguity*. Eventually, the presentation of the NS (bell) alone elicits the response of salivation. The bell is now no longer a neutral stimulus but elicits a response which is conditional on learning. It is therefore called a *conditional stimulus* (CS) and the response it elicits is a *conditional response* or *conditional reflex* (CR). As Figure 3.2 shows, the original UCR appears to have been transferred to the CS, as a result of which there is now an S-R link between the bell (CS) and salivation (CR).

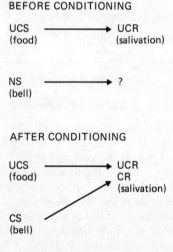

Figure 3.2   Classical conditioning

SAQ 35

A common experiment to show classical conditioning in humans is to blow a puff of air into their eyes to make them blink. The puff of air is preceded by a bell and eventually people blink to the sound of the bell alone. Identify:

NS   UCR
UCS   CR
CS

The next question is: what happens if the experimenter keeps presenting the bell on its own without any food? Eventually the dog will stop salivating when it hears the bell. This is known as *extinction*, because the learned response of salivating to the bell has been extinguished.

Pavlov (1927) also investigated whether, after conditioning a dog to salivate to a stimulus, it would respond in the same way to similar stimuli. A dog was conditioned to salivate to a previously neutral stimulus, in this case a drawing of a circle rather than the sound of a bell. When conditioning was complete the dog was presented with drawings of other shapes including an ellipse, a square, a triangle and a star. It responded by salivating to all of these shapes, as if the response of salivation had generalized from the original CS (the circle) to other stimuli, a process known as *generalization*. Moreover, the greater the similarity between the circle and the other shapes, the greater the amount of saliva produced by the animal.

Given that the dog is now salivating both to a circle and to an ellipse, if the circle continues to be paired with food while the ellipse is presented on its own without any food, the dog will end up by salivating only to the circle but not to the ellipse, i.e. it will learn to discriminate between them. *Discrimination* has been used as a technique to test the capacity of organisms to 'see' differences between stimuli. If the ellipse is too similar to a circle, the dog cannot learn to discriminate between the two because it cannot see any difference between the circle and the ellipse, although other organisms, e.g. humans, might be able to see a difference.

Key Notes 3.2

1 The components of classical conditioning are:

Neutral stimulus (NS) which does not elicit the reflex response before the experiment.

Unconditional stimulus (UCS) which elicits an *innate reflex response* (UCR).

Conditional stimulus (CS), the previously neutral stimulus, which now elicits a conditional learned response.

Conditional response (CR), a learned response to a previously neutral stimulus.

2 Conditioning occurs when the NS is paired with the UCS often enough for an association to be formed between them. Eventually the presentation of the NS (now CS) elicits the UCR (now CR).

3 Extinction results when a CS (e.g. bell) ceases to be paired with the UCS (e.g. food), so that the CS no longer elicits the CR (e.g. salivation).

4 Generalization occurs when other NS are similar enough to a CS for the CR to be generalized to them. Discrimination occurs when the organism discriminates between the CS and other similar stimuli, so that the CR occurs only to the CS.

3.3 OPERANT CONDITIONING

Diagnostic Questions for Section 3.3

1 What is the law of effect?
2 Define operant conditioning.
3 What factors lead to discrimination and stimulus control?
4 Give examples of shaping procedures.

The problem with classical conditioning is that it only accounts for the transfer of innate involuntary responses (e.g. salivation) from an unconditional stimulus (e.g. food) to a conditional stimulus (e.g. bell). It does not account for the acquisition of new responses which are not among the innate responses of the organism. Yet most of our learning consists of developing new responses and skills such as driving a car or playing chess. Where do these new behaviours come from if they are not innate reflexes in the first place?

The first attempt to demonstrate the learning of new responses was Thorndike's study of trial and error learning by cats (see Techniques Box M).

TECHNIQUES BOX M

Thorndike's Puzzle Box

A hungry cat is placed in a puzzle box, outside which is a dish of food. To get out to eat the food, the cat has to work a mechanical contrivance to open the door, such as a string attached to the door latch. When first put into the box the cat struggles and miaows as if trying to escape. During the course of this behaviour it accidentally pulls the string, the door opens and the cat walks out to eat the food. When put back in the box the cat again accidentally pulls the string, the door opens and it escapes to the food. Over a series of such trials the cat takes less and less time to pull the string to get out of the box.

Perhaps the most important aspect of Thorndike's work was his demonstration of motivational factors in learning. The cat might not have made such an effort to escape from the puzzle box had it not been hungry. This led Thorndike (1932) to develop his famous learning principle known as the *law of effect*. This states that learning occurs only if a response has some effect on the organism. If the effect of a response has pleasant consequences for the organism, then learning occurs through the strengthening of the connection between the stimulus and the response. If, on the other hand, a response has unpleasant consequences, then the behaviour is weakened.

This concept of learning was the basis for the learning theory developed by B. F. Skinner, the most famous proponent of modern behaviourism. Skinner distinguishes between two different kinds of learning. He refers to the first as *respondent behaviour* (often simply called respondents), which follows the pattern of classical conditioning when an organism learns to associate innate responses to new stimuli. Skinner was mainly interested in the second category of naturally emitted *operant behaviour*, natural in the sense that it is not directly elicited by a particular stimulus. Operant behaviour (often referred to simply as operants) can be conditioned according to the laws of *operant conditioning*.

Skinner's views about why learning occurs are similar to Thorndike's. If a response is followed by a reward this will increase the probability of that response occurring again. If rewards are given only after an animal has emitted a desired response, i.e. the reward is made contingent on that response, an experimenter should be able to modify any behaviour which is naturally emitted by an organism. Operant conditioning is sometimes also called *instrumental conditioning* because the behaviour of the animal is instrumental to obtaining the reward. Such a reward is known as a *reinforcement* because it acts to reinforce, i.e. increase, the desired response.

Over many years Skinner (1938, 1953, 1974) carried out experiments with rats and pigeons in order to demonstrate the laws of operant conditioning. An example is shown in Techniques Box N (p.52).

Although operant conditioning is the most usual type of conditioning, it is interesting that it tends to focus more on the response (R) and reinforcement than on the stimulus (S). In a Skinner Box, the stimulus might be considered to be the box as a whole including the lighted button. The reinforcement is the food which increases the pigeon's responses.

Skinner calls the lighted button a *discriminative stimulus* because the animal learns to peck the button only when it is lit up, i.e. it learns to discriminate situations in which a response will result in reinforcement. In this way, behaviour can be brought under *stimulus control*. For instance, if food only appears after pecking a red button but not after a blue button, the pigeon soon learns to discriminate between the red and blue buttons by pecking the red button only. An example of stimulus control in everyday life is a speeding driver who only slows down at the sight of a police car, thus showing that he can discriminate between the presence and absence of police cars!

TECHNIQUES BOX N

Conditioning in a Skinner Box

A hungry pigeon is put into a 'Skinner' box with a lighted button on the wall. At first the pigeon struts round the box, pecking here and there. Eventually it pecks at the lighted button and immediately a container of grain opens in the wall. The pigeon eats for a few seconds, but then the container closes. The pigeon again begins to strut about and peck randomly. Again it happens to peck the lighted button and again the food container opens for a few seconds. As time goes on the pigeon will cease its random pecking and, each time the food container closes, will immediately peck the lighted button (see Figure 3.3). The access to the food container has reinforced the button pecking behaviour by making it more likely that the pecking behaviour will be repeated.

Figure 3.3

SAQ 36

A child is in a school classroom. When he is quiet (reading or drawing), the teacher pays no attention to him. He throws a ball of paper at another child. The teacher tells him off. He starts reading but after a while throws something again. The teacher pays attention to him. After a time he frequently throws things.

Identify:
    the discriminative stimulus
    the different behaviours emitted
    the reinforcement
    the child's behaviour which was reinforced

One problem with operant conditioning is that it depends on behaviour being naturally emitted by the organism. But suppose you want to teach your dog to fetch your slippers. It would probably be a very long time before the dog happened to 'emit' the behaviour of picking up your slippers which you want to reinforce. In order to hurry along the learning process, Skinner developed the notion of *shaping* up the organism to produce a response. The method proceeds by rewarding naturally emitted behaviour which gradually approximates to the desired behaviour (see Techniques Box O).

TECHNIQUES BOX O

Shaping a Pigeon to Bowl

The hungry animal is put in a box with a ball and some ninepins. The arrival of food is signalled by the experimenter ringing a bell. As the bird wanders about it will sooner or later make a step towards the ball. As this is a step in the right direction the bell rings and the pigeon is rewarded with food. After eating, the bird will recommence its random trial and error movements around the box. As soon as the pigeon heads towards the ball it is again rewarded. As this pattern is repeated the pigeon has to go a little nearer the ball each time before it is reinforced until it has learned to walk up to the ball itself.

To get this to happen reinforcement is initially given for an approximate response but later is withheld for these responses and only presented again for behaviour which is closer to what the experimenter wants.

The next task is getting the bird's beak down on the floor next to the ball. As pigeons move, their heads bob up and down, so only downward movements are rewarded until the pigeon accidentally touches the ball with its beak. Later the bird's 'hitting' responses can be reinforced so that it knocks the ball straight down the alley instead of merely hitting it in any random direction. An experienced pigeon-handler can usually train a hungry pigeon to 'bowl' in less than an hour. (Training the animal to get a good score takes a little longer.)

SAQ 37
Why do you think the pigeon was first trained to associate a bell with food?

The technique of gradually shaping behaviour by giving and withholding reinforcement is the usual technique for training animals and has also been applied to humans. For example, it has been employed for modifying abnormal behaviour, known as *behaviour modification*. One such example involved the gradual shaping of verbal responses of a catatonic schizophrenic patient, who had been mute for nineteen years prior to the treatment. Through the careful shaping of her behaviour, by reinforcing approximations like opening her mouth, she progressed to making verbal requests and interacting freely with both staff and inmates (although one wonders whether other factors might not have been at work such as the friendly attention the patient was getting).

Key Notes 3.3

1 The law of effect is a theory developed by Thorndike to explain trial and error learning; responses which are rewarded are likely to be repeated, those which are punished to disappear.
2 Operant conditioning, as developed by Skinner, depends on the principle that learning occurs only if an organism's response is reinforced by a reinforcer.
3 Organisms learn to discriminate between stimuli in the presence of which reinforcement is given and other stimuli when no reinforcement appears. The animal is thus brought under the stimulus control of a discriminative stimulus.
4 Shaping is a method of training by which a response is shaped by the reinforcement of successive approximations to the desired behaviour.

3.4 COMPARISON BETWEEN CLASSICAL AND OPERANT CONDITIONING

Diagnostic Questions for Section 3.4

1 What types of behaviour can be classically or operantly conditioned?
2 What are the main differences in experimental procedures between classical and operant conditioning?
3 What role does reinforcement play in classical and operant conditioning?
4 List the main similarities between the two types of conditioning.

In classical conditioning the only kind of behaviour which can be conditioned is an innate involuntary reflex (UCR) which is already elicited by a stimulus (UCS). The UCR can be transferred to a neutral stimulus, thus becoming a conditional response (now CR) to an originally neutral stimulus (now CS). Although the original UCR has to be an innate reflex, it is possible for a CS-CR link to be transferred to another neutral stimulus. Once an animal has learnt to salivate to a bell this response (CR) can be transferred to a tone by pairing the bell and the tone. However, it is still the case that this is an innate response (e.g. salivation) that is being transferred from one stimulus to another.

In operant conditioning many kinds of behaviour which are emitted by an organism can be conditioned by reinforcement. However, the experimenter has to wait for an appropriate response before he can start shaping a new pattern of responses by applying and withdrawing reinforcement.

The experimental procedures for the two types of conditioning are quite different. In classical conditioning the organism has no control over the presentation of either UCS or CS. The bell and food appear whether the animal responds or not. In operant conditioning the responses of the organism determine whether a reinforcement is given. Food is only presented if the animal responds, so reinforcement is contingent upon the animal producing the correct response. The two procedures can be compared as shown in Figure 3.4.

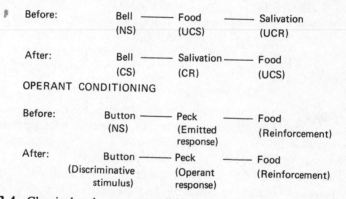

CLASSICAL CONDITIONING

Before: Bell ———— Food ———— Salivation
         (NS)   (UCS)   (UCR)

After: Bell ———— Salivation ———— Food
         (CS)   (CR)   (UCS)

OPERANT CONDITIONING

Before: Button ———— Peck ———— Food
         (NS)   (Emitted   (Reinforcement)
                      response)

After: Button ———— Peck ———— Food
         (Discriminative (Operant   (Reinforcement)
         stimulus)   response)

Figure 3.4 Classical and operant conditioning compared

In both cases a neutral stimulus (bell or button) and a rewarding stimulus (like food) are presented by the experimenter. However, in classical conditioning the food plays an initiating role as a UCS which elicits the innate UCR (salivation) which later becomes the CR to the CS (bell). In operant conditioning the rewarding stimulus plays the role of a subsequent reinforcer which increases the probability of emitting the operant response again in the presence of the discriminative stimulus (button).

You should note, however, that despite these apparently clear theoretical and procedural differences between classical and operant conditioning, what actually happens in experiments is not as distinct as it may seem. Often both classical and operant conditioning may be occurring in the same situation, as when a pigeon is classically conditioned to transfer a response from a lighted button to a bell.

There has also been a lot of argument about whether the food in a classical conditioning experiment is acting not only as a UCS but also as a reward. In fact, one interpretation of the dog's behaviour is that the bell is a signal that a reward is coming; so it gets ready to eat the food by salivating. It has been argued that salivation makes the food more rewarding but in any case salivation can be thought of as an anticipatory response to the food. Evidence in favour of this view is that it is very difficult, if not impossible, to condition a response if the food is presented before the bell, a procedure known as *backward conditioning*.

Other similarities between classical and operant conditioning are that both are susceptible to the same processes of extinction and discrimination (stimulus control) when rewards are withheld in the presence of certain stimuli.

SAQ 38
Which of the following statements are true of classical conditioning and/or operant conditioning?
(a) an organism's response is not instrumental in obtaining reinforcement
(b) naturally emitted behaviours may be conditioned
(c) reinforcement depends on the organism emitting the correct response
(d) a stimulus becomes a signal for reinforcement

Key Notes 3.4

1 Classical conditioning is limited to transferring elicited responses (innate reflexes) from one stimulus to another. In operant conditioning many freely occurring behaviours can be conditioned.

2 The main difference in experimental procedures is that in classical conditioning the UCS and CS are presented regardless of the animal's responses. In operant conditioning the reinforcement is contingent on the animal making a particular response.

3 In classical conditioning a rewarding stimulus like food acts as an UCS to elicit the UCR. In operant conditioning a rewarding stimulus like food acts as a reinforcer which affects the probability of the response which occurred just prior to the reinforcement.

4 Both classical and operant conditioning can occur in the same experimental situation. In both cases a previously neutral stimulus acts as a signal of a reward. In operant conditioning the animal has to do something to obtain the reward whereas in classical conditioning the CR appears to be an anticipatory response to a forthcoming reward. In both types of conditioning, withholding rewards leads to extinction and discrimination between rewarded and non-rewarded responses.

3.5 REWARDS AND PUNISHMENTS

Diagnostic Questions for Section 3.5

1 Differentiate between types of reinforcement which increase the probability of making a response and those which decrease it.
2 What are the effects of positive and negative reinforcement?
3 How does punishment work?
4 Why is avoidance learning so effective?
5 What are the advantages and disadvantages of punishment?

Stemming from Thorndike's 'law of effect', *reinforcement* is defined as anything which increases the likelihood of an organism repeating a response. *Positive reinforcement* includes conventional rewards like food and anything else which increases the probability of responding. The removal of an unpleasant reinforcer can also increase the probability of a prior response. This is known as *negative reinforcement* because it is the removal of an aversive stimulus which is 'rewarding' to the animal. An example would be training a rat to make an escape response like jumping from one box to another when the floor of the first box is electrified to give the animal a shock. The removal of the shock acts as a negative reinforcer to condition the jumping responses. It still counts as reinforcement because it increases the probability of making a response, in this case jumping.

In operant conditioning, it is possible for the rat to make a response which will result in the removal of the shock. In classical conditioning, a bell and shock may be paired but in conditions in which the shock is unavoidable, e.g. it is administered through a wire attached to the dog's leg. The dog very quickly learns to transfer its fear and anxiety responses to the bell but there is nothing it can do to escape the shock. A condition in which an animal finds that it cannot do anything to terminate an aversive stimulus can lead to *learned helplessness*. It was found that dogs which had been exposed to unavoidable shock later made no attempt to learn a response even though it would have enabled them to avoid a shock (Seligman, 1971). This has been used as an explanation of why some people 'give up' the effort to take action to influence outcomes in their life.

One very effective type of learning is known as *avoidance learning*. In this situation an animal can make a response like jumping away from an electrified section of a box even before the shock occurs. The animal will continue to make avoidance responses over very long periods. One plausible explanation is that, by avoiding the shock, the animal never has the chance to discover whether the shock is still there. Consequently, the behaviour can never be extinguished since the rat never risks exposing itself to the experience of discovering whether the box is still a discriminative stimulus for the occurance of shock. For instance, someone who has had a bad experience in marriage may learn to avoid that stimulus situation and so never discovers that not all marriages are 'paired' with unpleasant experiences.

Punishment is defined as the opposite of reinforcement since it is designed to reduce or eliminate a response rather than increase it. Like reinforcement, punishment can work either by directly applying an unpleasant stimulus like a shock after a response, or by removing a potentially rewarding stimulus, for instance, by deducting pocket money to punish undesirable behaviour. In both cases the aim is that the organism, animal or human, should stop doing the punished response; in other words, there will be a decreased probability of the response occurring again.

SAQ 39
Fill in the table below to indicate whether the presentation or removal of each type of stimulus, pleasant or unpleasant, is likely to increase or decrease the probability of responding. Which boxes refer to reinforcement and which to punishment?

	presentation	removal
pleasant	(a)	(b)
unpleasant	(c)	(d)

SAQ 40
Looking back to SAQ 36 in Section 3.3, did the teacher's negative reaction to the child's behaviour act as a positive reinforcement or as a punisher? What might have been the result if the teacher had ignored the child's disruptive behaviour?

Punishment is often thought to be less effective than positive reinforcement because it works by eliminating unsatisfactory responses rather than conditioning desired responses. Harsh punishments can cause so much anxiety that they inhibit all responses. However, punishment can obviously have beneficial effects in cases where it is vital for an organism to learn quickly to stop making a response to a dangerous stimulus.

SAQ 41
Is there anything in common between punishment and extinction?

Key Notes 3.5

1 Reinforcement is defined as anything which increases the probability of a response; punishment as anything which decreases the probability of a response.

2 Positive reinforcement occurs when a response is followed by a rewarding stimulus, negative reinforcement when a response is followed by the removal of an aversive stimulus. In both cases the probability of a response occurring again is increased.

3 Punishment occurs when a response is followed either by an aversive stimulus or by removal of a reward. In both cases the probability of a response occurring again is decreased.

4 In avoidance learning an organism learns to avoid an aversive stimulus. An avoidance response tends never to get extinguished because, by avoiding the aversive stimulus, the organism never discovers whether the aversive stimulus is still paired with the stimulus situation.

5 Punishment eliminates behaviour rather than training desirable responses and it can cause excessive anxiety. Punishment may be useful for rapid elimination of a response to a dangerous stimulus.

3.6 SCHEDULES OF REINFORCEMENT

Diagnostic Questions for Section 3.6

1 What is the difference between continuous and partial reinforcement?
2 Name four kinds of partial reinforcement schedules.
3 What is 'Humphreys' paradox?

So far it has been assumed that reinforcement is an all-or-none affair. Learning occurs if a response is reinforced; extinguished if it is not. But, of course, in real life we are not reinforced every time we do something. To take just one example, workers are paid once a week or month, not every time they make a desirable response from their employer's point of view.

Reinforcement which is presented every time a response is made is known as *continuous reinforcement*. The presentation of reinforcement only after some responses but not others is known as *partial reinforcement* or *intermittent reinforcement*. Skinner carried out a long series of experiments, mainly with rats and pigeons, to study the effects of different *reinforcement schedules*.

The animals' responses are recorded on a continuously moving sheet along which a pen makes a mark. Each response appears as a vertical notch so that an upward slope on the paper indicates that the animal is making a lot of responses whereas a flat horizontal line means that the animal is not responding at all. These are known as *cumulative records* of an animal's progress. In Techniques Box P the figures show cumulative records with dashes when reinforcements were given.

TECHNIQUES BOX P

Partial Reinforcement Schedules

Fixed-Interval Schedule (FI)

Under this schedule, reinforcement is given at regular fixed intervals of time. In a one-minute fixed-interval schedule (FI-1′), for example, the organism is reinforced at the end of each minute, provided that the animal has made at least one response during that period. So, to receive its maximum reward, the organism only needs to respond once a minute. When reinforced in this way, it is found that after each reward the organism pauses for a while before starting to respond again. Figure 3.5 shows this pattern of responding when reinforcements are given at minute intervals (shown by the dashes in the figure).

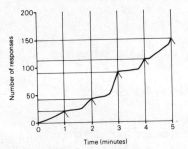

Figure 3.5 Cumulative record of lever presses by a rat on a one-minute fixed-interval schedule.

Variable-Interval Schedule (VI)

In this schedule, reinforcement is given at semi-random intervals, sometimes after short intervals and sometimes after long ones. A variable-interval schedule of one minute (VI-1′) means that some rewards may occur after 30 seconds, some after 90 seconds, but the average interval is 1 minute. The effect is a more consistent rate of responding but still a tendency to respond more quickly as time passes and a reward becomes more likely (see Figure 3.6).

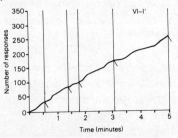

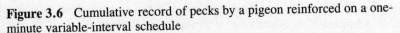

Figure 3.6 Cumulative record of pecks by a pigeon reinforced on a one-minute variable-interval schedule

SAQ 42
In Figure 3.6, after approximately how long did the pigeon receive its third reinforcement and how many pecks had the pigeon made altogether by that time?

Fixed-Ratio Schedule (FR)
A reinforcement is given after a fixed number of responses. For example,
a FR-50 schedule means that a pigeon is reinforced after every 50 lever
presses. The result of this schedule is a very high rate of responding with
short pauses after reinforcement followed by a rapid burst of activity until
the next reinforcement (see Figure 3.7). This time the reinforcement dashes
are related to the number of responses up the vertical axis.

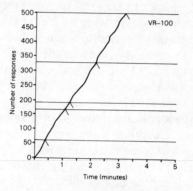

Figure 3.7 Cumulative record of pecks by a pigeon reinforced for every
50 pecks, on a fixed-ratio schedule

Variable-Ratio Schedule (VR)
This schedule presents reinforcement after a variable number of responses,
sometimes after a few responses and sometimes after many. A VR-100
means that reinforcement may follow after 10 pecks or after 190 pecks, as
long as the average is 100. Variable-ratio schedules produce continuously
high rates of responding (see Figure 3.8).

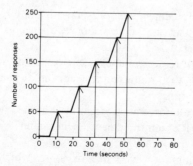

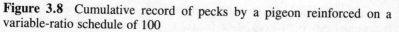

Figure 3.8 Cumulative record of pecks by a pigeon reinforced on a
variable-ratio schedule of 100

You will remember that withdrawal of reinforcement extinguishes a response, so we might expect that responses which are only reinforced on some but not all occasions are more likely to get extinguished. Contrary to this expectation, extinction is in fact much slower when a response has been intermittently reinforced than when it has been continuously reinforced. A partially reinforced response persists for much longer even when it stops being reinforced altogether. This result so surprised psychologists that they called it 'Humphreys' paradox', after Lloyd G. Humphreys, who first demonstrated the special resistance to extinction of partially reinforced responses.

One plausible explanation for this is that an organism on a continuous reinforcement schedule comes to 'expect' reinforcement all the time so, the moment reinforcement stops, it becomes 'disheartened' and stops responding. But, if an animal gets used to a schedule in which reinforcements only happen intermittently, absence of reinforcement does not necessarily mean that reinforcement will not occur again in the future, so it is worthwhile continuing to respond to see if it does. This is particularly noticeable with the variable schedules since the animal will have got used to waiting for long periods (variable interval) or making lots of responses (variable ratio) before receiving a response. After a variable-ratio schedule a rat or pigeon will go on responding for a very long time without further reinforcements. You should note the 'un-behaviourist' tone of these speculations which depend on assuming that the animal has internal mental processes like 'expecting' and 'getting used to'.

SAQ 43
Which of the reinforcement schedules are operating in (a) weekly wages, (b) piece work, (c) a fruit machine? What patterns of responding would be expected to follow in each case from Skinner's results?

Key Notes 3.6

1 In continuous reinforcement every response is reinforced; in partial (intermittent) reinforcement only some responses are reinforced according to the following schedules.

2 *Fixed-Interval* (FI): reinforcements occur at regular time intervals.
Variable-Interval (VI): reinforcements occur at random time intervals around an average time.
Fixed-ratio (FR): reinforcements occur after a fixed number of responses.
Variable-ratio (VR): reinforcements occur after a random number of responses around an average.

3 According to 'Humphreys' paradox', responses which have been intermittently reinforced take longer to extinguish than responses which have been continuously reinforced. This is probably due to the fact that intermittent

schedules accustom the organism to responding without a reward, especially variable schedules.

3.7 THEORIES OF REINFORCEMENT

Diagnostic Questions for Section 3.7

1 Distinguish between primary and secondary reinforcement.
2 Comment on different explanations of how secondary reinforcers acquire their reinforcing properties.
3 Evaluate Hull's drive theory of reinforcement.

In previous sections the emphasis has been on the effects of reinforcement on responses. Strict behaviourists like Skinner still define reinforcers as anything which can be shown to increase the probability of a response. Nevertheless theories have been put forward to explain why reinforcers actually work.

One theory of reinforcement states that reinforcers are effective because they satisfy the biological needs of an organism, such as hunger or thirst. This is known as the *need reduction theory of reinforcement*. Such innate reinforcers are known as *primary reinforcement* because their reinforcing value is automatic; the animal does not have to learn that food or drink are reinforcing.

Because of the fact that humans are often reinforced by less direct means, it has been suggested that there must be secondary reinforcers such as smiles, praise and money. Behaviourists claim that *secondary reinforcement* works because, at some time in an organism's life, a secondary reinforcer has been paired with a primary reinforcer and so has taken over the reinforcing value of the primary reinforcer.

SAQ 44
An example might be a child's pleasure at getting good reports. How could this be explained by classical conditioning? What would be the NS UCS UCR CS CR?

Some secondary reinforcers may indeed acquire their reinforcing value through classical conditioning, by being presented in association with a primary reinforcer; for instance, the mother's smile when feeding a child may become a secondary reinforcer. But there are also examples where the relationship seems to be more instrumental in that the organism can only obtain a primary reinforcer by first acquiring a secondary reinforcer. An example of this kind of operant conditioning is given in Techniques Box Q.

TECHNIQUES BOX Q

Conditioning of a Secondary Reinforcer

Wolfe (1936) conducted a study to investigate how effective secondary reinforcement could be in training chimpanzees. Chimpanzees, like babies, are naturally indifferent to money. A vending machine was placed in the corner of the chimpanzees' cage, which would produce a grape on the insertion of a poker chip. After the chimps had learned this association, Wolfe found that he could teach them to do other tasks such as pressing a lever to obtain poker chips as reinforcement. Even when the vending machine was not present the monkeys would still work to accumulate chips which they could use later to operate the machine.

SAQ 45
In this experiment what was the primary reinforcer and the secondary reinforcer?

A form of secondary reinforcement, using tokens, has been widely employed by psychologists in the treatment of maladaptive behaviour, ranging from very disruptive children in the classroom to chronically psychotic adults in hospitals. The system used is known as a *token economy programme* (TEP). In order to 'shape' desired behaviour, e.g. that patients take care of their appearance or speak to others, use is made of positive reinforcement, coupled with removal of rewards to eliminate undesirable behaviour. Because of the obvious difficulties arising from trying to reinforce every desired behaviour with primary reinforcers such as food and drink, tokens (usually small plastic discs) are used which can be exchanged for primary reinforcers such as food or drink, or watching TV.

SAQ 46
Why do you think watching TV is a primary reinforcer?

One problem is that when patients leave the hospital they often revert to maladaptive behaviour. One of the striking things about most human behaviour is the extent to which it is influenced by secondary reinforcers which seem to have lost all connection with primary reinforcement; for instance, the person who hoards money or spends it on other secondary reinforcers like expensive clothes or prestigious furniture. People who have been hospitalized for long periods are likely to be confused when they find that their actions are no longer automatically rewarded by 'tokens', which in any case are non-negotiable in everyday life.

A more sophisticated version of the theory that reinforcement is based on an organism's needs was proposed by the famous learning theorist Clark Hull, who was particularly influential in the 1940s. Hull believed that biological needs are mediated through drives. *Drives* are caused by a primary need such as hunger or thirst; reinforcers such as food and drink work because they reduce drive states. This is known as the *drive reduction theory of reinforcement*.

The importance of the concept of drive for Hull was that he attempted to produce a theory of S-R learning, taking into account all the factors which can be shown to affect responses. Hull (1943) postulated what he called *intervening variables* to account for the way responses become linked to stimuli. He called them intervening variables because they intervene between stimulus inputs and responses. Figure 3.9 shows how factors like drive (D), which depends on how long the animal has been kept hungry; habit strength (sHr), which depends on the number of reinforced S-R pairings; incentive (K), which depends on the size of the reward, are related to sEr, the excitory potential which produces the response. The greater the drive, habit strength (i.e. learning) and incentive, the more likely the organism is to make a response.

One important point to notice is that these intervening variables are strictly tied to observable conditions, like the number of hours since the rat was last fed. Moreover, although it looks as if the 'Black Box' representing the mind has now been filled up with internal mechanisms like drives and habits, Hull did not commit himself to the actual existence of 'mental' psychological processes. By assigning numbers like hours of food deprivation or weight of food, Hull derived mathematical equations which he hoped would predict every detail of a rat's behaviour. This bold ambition had to be abandoned when it was found that even a white rat's behaviour is too variable to predict exactly, much less human behaviour.

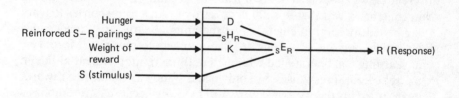

Figure 3.9 Hull's intervening variables

SAQ 47
Can you see why 'drive' theories are often circular? What is the evidence that a drive exists for watching TV?

Key Notes 3.7

1 Primary reinforcement depends on primary reinforcers which are innately satisfying to the organism, e.g. food. Secondary reinforcement depends on

secondary reinforcers which are only satisfying as a result of previous learning, e.g. money.

2 Secondary reinforcers may acquire their reinforcing properties through being paired with innate primary reinforcers (classical conditioning) or by being instrumental in obtaining a primary reward (operant conditioning). However, it is often very difficult to trace the connecting links between a secondary reinforcer and an original primary reinforcer, particularly when it comes to explaining human behaviour.

3 Hull proposed that reinforcers work because they reduce drives. One difficulty is that often the only evidence for a drive is that an organism is reinforced by a reward, which it is assumed must have reduced a drive for that reward.

3.8 WHAT IS LEARNT?

Diagnostic Questions for Section 3.8

1 Outline evidence in favour of Tolman's theory about the learning of cognitive maps.
2 What evidence is there that some S-R links are more natural than others in evolutionary terms?
3 Evaluate the current status of learning theories.

E. C. Tolman, another famous learning theorist who wrote in the 1930s and 1940s, did not dispute the existence of reinforcement but had very different views about what kind of learning is being reinforced. Tolman's main contention was that it is not necessarily particular responses that are strengthened by reinforcement; what the animal learns are expectancies about which stimulus situations are likely to lead to rewards. Moreover, some learning can be initiated without a definite reinforcement, although actual behavioural responses will only occur if they can achieve a reward. Tolman called his theory an *S-S theory of learning* because of its emphasis on which stimulus situations lead to rewarding or punishing stimuli, rather than on specific S-R links. His theory is also known as a *sign learning theory* because stimuli act as 'signs' of likely situations which might lead to rewards (Tolman, 1932).

SAQ 48
What has Tolman's S-S theory got in common with Skinner's notion of a discriminative stimulus?

Techniques Box R describes a typical experiment by Tolman and his colleagues which is designed to show that animals can learn things about their environment without being reinforced for particular responses.

TECHNIQUES BOX R

Latent Learning

Tolman and Honzik (1930) carried out an experiment in which three groups of rats, A, B and C, were run daily in a complex maze. Group A were given a food reinforcement when they reached the goal box at the end of the maze. Group B were allowed to explore the maze but, when the rats reached the goal box, they were removed with no reinforcement. Group C were treated in the same way as Group B for the first ten days and then given reinforcement for the remaining seven days. As you can see in Figure 3.10, all the groups learned something as the days went by since they made fewer errors in reaching the goal box. However, the reinforced group A learned more rapidly than the two non-reinforced groups B and C. With the introduction of food on the eleventh day, however, the third group C immediately started performing as well as the reinforced group A.

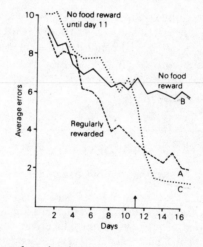

Figure 3.10 Latent learning in rats

Tolman claimed that the Group C rats must have been developing an internal *cognitive map* of the maze during the first ten days, including information about dead ends and incorrect pathways which they could put to use when a reward was introduced. The important point is that the rats' learning must have been in the form of an *internal representation* of their experience of the maze, since their observable behaviour prior to the reward gave no sign of learning.

Other experiments have shown that, if a maze is flooded after rats have learned a path to food, they will easily swim their way there rather than stick to the actual running responses which were originally reinforced.

Certainly Tolman's ideas are more in tune with present-day thinking — that what is learnt are expectations which guide behaviour in certain situations. It would be very uneconomic if we had to learn a specific pattern of responses for each particular stimulus rather than assessing a situation as a whole. Imagine responding in exactly the same way to a 'bell' regardless of whether we were expecting a fire drill or not.

One difference between Hull and Tolman is that, although they both postulated internal mechanisms inside the Black Box, Hull wanted to tie these very specifically to observable stimulus inputs and responses. Tolman was prepared to talk more loosely — some would say more persuasively — about mental concepts like cognitive maps and expectancies as being necessary to explain even the behaviour of rats.

SAQ 49
How is the link between stimulus situation, learned response and reinforcement handled in (a) classical conditioning (b) Skinnerian operant conditioning (c) Tolman's theory?

Another issue concerning 'what is learnt' is that classical behaviourists often assumed that any species could learn any response. More recently psychologists have begun to take notice of what biologists have been saying about the behaviour of animals in their natural habitats. The aim has been to show that some S-R linkings are more or less natural because they are relevant to survival.

TECHNIQUES BOX S

Natural Pairings of Stimuli

Garcia and Koelling (1966) designed an experiment in which two groups of rats were given a saccharin solution to drink and simultaneously a bell was sounded. Group 1 received a shock immediately after drinking. Group 2 received an injection that made them feel nausea 30 minutes after drinking. Later both groups were tested for their willingness to drink in the presence of each of the cues potentially predictive of harm : noise of the bell or taste of saccharin. Group 1, which received shocks, were reluctant to drink anything (saccharin or pure water) in the presence of the bell, indicating that they had formed an association between the bell and the shock. However, in the absence of the bell they were not reluctant to drink saccharin water, indicating they had formed no association between taste and the shock. Conversely, Group 2, which received a nauseous injection, were reluctant to drink saccharin water, indicating that they had formed an association between taste and nausea. However, they were willing to drink pure water even in the presence of the bell, indicating that they had formed no association between the bell and nausea. In summary, rats easily associate (a) sound and shock, and (b) taste and nausea, but not (c) taste and shock, nor (d) sound and nausea. The argument is that it is important for animals to respond to noise as a signal of immediate external danger and to identify the taste of something nauseous. The opposite pairings simply don't make evolutionary sense.

It is interesting that the S-R pairs chosen by early behaviourists were all possible ones, although there may, of course, have been some trial and error attempts before finding that bells and food, buttons and pecks are compatible pairs. Nevertheless, while certain restrictions may be true of animals, one of the amazing things about humans is their extreme flexibility in learning bizarre and often damaging habits which are certainly not conducive to our survival.

Finally, there are experiments which indicate that animals take a more active role in learning than would be indicated by the notion of reinforcing specific S-R links. In Kohler's (1925) famous experiments, apes showed insight into problems, producing novel solutions like picking up a stick to pull in a banana out of reach. It has also been shown (Harlow, Harlow and Meyer, 1950) that monkeys will solve puzzles without any apparent reward at all.

One conclusion that can be drawn, even from a consideration of learning in the behaviourist tradition, is that learning is a very complex business. The 1940s and 1950s were the heyday of learning research. Since then work on learning has tended to diverge in two directions. Behaviourists in the Skinnerian tradition have continued to concentrate on an extremely careful analysis of the intricate relationships between responses and reinforcement. The types of behaviour studied have been widened to include *behaviour therapy*, in which undesirable behaviours in patients are extinguished and desirable behaviours reinforced.

One difficulty with applying S-R theory to human behaviour is that it is not at all easy to identify exactly what is acting as a stimulus and what as a reinforcement. Since the chain between a stimulus and an ultimate response is long and complex, definitions of stimuli and reinforcers often tend to be circular. If a child writes a school essay when asked to by a teacher, it can be postulated that the teacher's request is the stimulus and that the child produces the response because of a drive to obtain high grades. But what independent evidence is there for such conditioning mechanisms except the behaviour itself? If the child had responded by not turning up at school, some other stimulus and reinforcers could easily be invented to account for this behaviour: for instance, an avoidance response to the aversive stimulus of having to write the essay or going fishing to reduce a boredom drive.

This has led psychologists to take up Tolman's idea that learning involves changes in mental representations rather than direct behaviour. These more mental aspects of learning have become the focus of attention in cognitive psychology, a topic which will be covered in a later volume in this series. However, it must be admitted that theories of how and why learning occurs have tended to be neglected in the pursuit of behavioural analysis on the one hand and mental representations on the other.

SAQ 50
Is Tolman's theory a top-down or bottom-up theory?

Key Notes 3.8

1 Tolman's S-S theory that animals learn internal representations of their environment (cognitive maps) rather than specific S-R links is supported by latent learning experiments.
2 Recent experiments have shown that it is not always possible to condition arbitrary S-R pairs. Some pairings are easier to condition because they are adaptive in an animal's habitat.
3 The current status of learning research is that it has diverged in two directions: analysis of behaviour in the Skinnerian tradition and cognitive psychologists' interest in mental representations of experience.

READING GUIDE

General Reading

WALKER, S. (1984), *Learning Theory and Behaviour Modification*, London, Methuen.
BOLLES, R. C. (1978), *Learning Theory*, New York, Holt, Rinehart and Winston.
MILLER, G. A. (1972), *Psychology: The Science of Mental Life*, Harmondsworth, Penguin, Chapters 12 and 13.
OPEN UNIVERSITY *DS262 Introduction to Psychology*, Unit 3.

Reading for each Section

Section 3.1: *DS262*, Unit 3, Section 1
Section 3.2: *DS262*, Unit 3, Section 2
            Miller, Chapter 12.

Section 3.3: *DS262*, Unit 3, Sections 3.1, 3.2, 3.3, 3.4.
Section 3.4: *DS262*, Unit 3, Section 3.7.
Section 3.5: *DS262*, Unit 3, Sections 3.5, 3.6.
Section 3.6: *DS262*, Unit 3, Section 4.2
Section 3.7: *DS262*, Unit 3, Sections 4.1, 6.1.
Section 3.8: *DS262*, Sections 5, 6, 7.

4

Memory Module

LINK FROM LEARNING TO MEMORY

To an outsider it might seem that learning and memory are one and the same thing. When we learn things we store them in memory; tests of memory like exams are taken as evidence of learning. In psychology, however, learning and memory have tended to be studied as separate topics. The earliest memory experiments done during the first decades of this century were influenced by the behaviourist tradition. Items to be remembered were thought of as stimulus inputs and recalls as responses. However, most of the later research done from the 1950s onwards stemmed from the information processing model described in Section 2.1 of the Attention Module, the aim being to specify the flow of information through a series of stages from input to final recall.

One advantage of behaviourism is that the same theoretical conceptions, experimental methods and procedures are common to everyone working in the field. In memory research the opposite has occurred. The 'grand' theories, which it was hoped would explain all kinds of learning in terms of the laws of conditioning, has given way to a fragmentation of minor theories. In turn, this has led to many different kinds of experimental procedures, each designed to illuminate one particular aspect of the memory process.

One final point to notice is that we will not be presenting the various lines of memory research in their historical order as outlined above. Instead, research will be described according to the stages of the information processing model, starting with input processes and only then going on to deal with storage processes.

General Diagnostic Questions for Memory

1 What is the role of memory in an information processing model? (Section 4.1)
2 Describe the characteristics and functions of sensory memory. (Section 4.2)
3 What conclusions can be drawn about STM from Peterson and Peterson's experiment? (Section 4.3)
4 Evaluate evidence for the interference theory of forgetting. (Section 4.4)
5 Are STM and LTM separate memory stores? (Section 4.5)

6 What are the implications of working memory and levels of processing for a multistore model of memory? (Section 4.6)
7 Discuss the role of organizational strategies in memory. (Section 4.7)

4.1 A MULTISTORE MODEL OF MEMORY

Diagnostic Questions for Section 4.1

1 What role does memory play in human behaviour?
2 What is the multistore model of memory?

In order to demonstrate the importance of memory, think about everything you did between getting up this morning and sitting down to breakfast. You probably included activities such as washing, dressing, calling the children, making the coffee (plus about a hundred other things!). Memory played a part in every one of these tasks − for instance, you had to remember the way to get to the bathroom, the order in which clothes should be put on (underwear before top wear), your children's names as well as remembering to call them. The important point to notice is that memory is not just a store of facts; it contains everything you know about interacting with the world. One way of conceptualizing *memory* is to think of it as a system for registering, storing and ultimately retrieving internal representations of events, including plans for the future.

It is obvious from what we have said that memory incorporates everything we know about human life and behaviour, but how have psychologists attempted to study memory? Basically they have tried to limit the kinds of memories studied in two main ways.

(i) The materials to be remembered are usually very simple (list of words and digits). This makes it easy to measure memory in terms of number of trials to learn, number of items recalled correctly and forgetting as measured by errors.

(ii) Memory has been considered as part of an information processing model of the kind described in Section 2.1 of the Attention Module. In a model of this kind, perception and attention processes control input of information; memory processes store information for retrieval and output.

One division within memory storage processes which has been extremely influential is a distinction between short-term memory (STM) and long-term memory (LTM). An example often given is the difference between remembering a telephone number you have just looked up for long enough to dial it and recalling an incident from your childhood.

SAQ 51
Which of the following are examples of short-term memory (STM) or long-term memory (LTM)?
(a) Recalling the number plate of a car long enough to write it down.
(b) Remembering the position of the gears in your car.
(c) Doing mental arithmetic.
(d) Memorizing a part for a school play.
(e) Recognizing a friend you haven't seen for years.

The notion of a dichotomy between short-term memory (STM) and long-term memory (LTM) has led psychologists to develop a *multistore model of memory*, multistore because it postulates several different stores within memory. A typical version is that proposed by Atkinson and Shriffrin (1968) which has provided a framework for much memory research. A simplified version is shown in Figure 4.1, which also includes sensory memory (SM). We will use the multistore model as a framework for introducing work on various stages in memory before going on to question whether such clear-cut divisions are actually reflected in human memory.

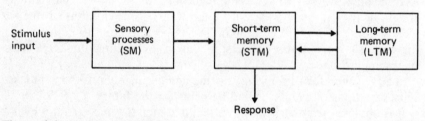

Figure 4.1   Multistore model of memory

SAQ 52
Look back to the general information processing model in Figure 2.1 in Section 2.1 of the Attention Module. How does the multistore model of memory fit into that model?

Key Notes 4.1

1 Memory is the repository where everything is stored that we need to know to interact with the environment.
2 The multistore model of memory divides memory into a series of stages including sensory memory (SM), short-term memory (STM) and long-term memory (LTM).

4.2 SENSORY MEMORY

Diagnostic Questions for Section 4.2

1 Define sensory memory, iconic memory and echoic memory.
2 Describe Sperling's cued partial report experimental procedure.
3 What are the functions of a rapidly decaying sensory memory?

It may seem rather odd to include a section on *sensory memory* (or *sensory registration* as it is sometimes called) when we have already had two modules, one on perception and the other on attention, both of which were concerned with how we perceive and attend to input. In the Perception Module, the main concern was with how information from our senses is organized so that we can perceive and recognize objects. In the Attention Module, research was directed to the question of how we filter out certain aspects of sensory information for full attention and analysis. In this Memory Module, researchers have been interested in how sensory information is retained in order for it to be entered into short-term memory. All this provides a telling example of how researchers often study the same processes from different points of view.

In memory research you will find sensory memory also called *iconic memory* (Neisser, 1967). We have used the term sensory memory (SM) because iconic memory refers only to visual input; the equivalent term for auditory input is *echoic memory*. These terms reflect the very transitory nature of SM; *icon* is a Greek word for image and echoic describes the way auditory input echoes in our ears.

A number of studies in the 1960s, stemming from a classic experiment by Sperling (1960), have demonstrated the existence of a visual sensory memory (iconic memory) capable of holding items for rather less than a second (see Techniques Box T) (p.76).

SAQ 53
What can be concluded about the capacity and duration of SM from Sperling's experiment?

What might the function of such a rapidly decaying sensory memory be? Coltheart, Lea and Thompson (1974) argue that the momentary retention of visual input allows us to select which aspects of input should go on to the next stage of the memory process. It also allows us to scan the whole of the visual environment within iconic memory or, to give an auditory example, it allows us to hold in echoic memory the first words of a sentence while the remaining words come in.

This interpretation of SM is similar to Neisser's notion of pre-attentive processes which continually monitor sensory information in the environment, as described in Section 2.6 of the Attention Module. As discussed in the Perception and Attention Modules, processing of sensory infor-

---

TECHNIQUES BOX T

Sperling's Sensory Memory Experiments

An array of letters is presented to a subject for just 50 msec (1/20th of a second) in a *tachistoscope*, which is a device for presenting stimuli for extremely brief periods measured in milliseconds (1/1000th of a second). The presentation is so fast that subjects don't have time to scan the whole array. Immediately after the brief exposure subjects are asked to name as many as possible of the letters they have seen. This is known as the *whole report (non-cued) condition*. Try this by glancing at the letters below and immediately putting your hand over them. How many can you remember?

R T K M
H L B F
S J W D

Typically subjects can only report four or five of the twelve items. However, they often say that they are sure they have seen more items than they are actually able to recall. Sperling assumed that this was caused by a limit on the number of items subjects could hold in STM for reporting rather than a limit on the number they could register originally. In order to circumvent the memory limitation, Sperling devised an experiment which would indicate the number of letters registered by the subject without requiring him to report more items than he could remember.

The technique he used was the *partial report condition*. Immediately after presentation of the stimulus array, Sperling presented a high, medium or low tone. Subjects had previously been instructed to report the contents of the top row of letters after the high tone, the middle row after the medium tone, and the bottom row after the low tone. Since the cue did not appear until after the array had disappeared, if subjects were able to select cued items for partial report, this must mean that all items were available as an image from which the items in the appropriate row could be selected for report. The argument is that, since subjects could report three out of four of the items in any particular cued row, they must have had available three items from each of the three rows, i.e. nine items out of the original twelve (75 per cent). This compares with the estimate of only four items out of twelve (25 per cent) obtained from the uncued whole report condition. The larger percentage (75 per cent) is taken to be a truer measure of capacity.

Sperling went on to show that, if the cue is delayed for more than about half a second, the advantage for partial report is lost, indicating that cued items can no longer be selected from sensory memory because the letters have decayed from SM.

---

mation is largely unconscious, so the registration of items in sensory memory can only be deduced from experiments like Sperling's. You should also note that Sperling assumes that, in the whole report condition, a bottleneck occurs in STM so that not all the items registered in SM can be reported by subjects. In the partial report condition the three or four items in each cued row can be passed straight through STM for output.

SAQ 54
Look back to Figure 2.3 in Section 2.2 of the Attention Module. Where would Broadbent's sensory buffer and limited capacity processor be placed in the multistore model in Figure 4.1 of this module?

Key Notes 4.2

1 Sensory memory (SM) is a term which refers to the very short term retention of information registered by the senses. It is known as iconic memory for visual inputs and echoic memory for auditory inputs.

2 By comparing the number of items reported from the whole array (whole report condition) and from each cued row (partial report condition), Sperling estimated that 75 per cent of items are registered in sensory memory, i.e. nine out of an array of twelve items. The duration of SM is estimated at less than one second because after that time cueing has no effect.

3 Sensory memory allows us to register briefly several inputs from the environment from which to select items for further storage.

4.3 SHORT-TERM MEMORY

Diagnostic Questions for Section 4.3

1 What does memory span measure?
2 Describe the Peterson and Peterson experiment and discuss two possible interpretations for their results.
3 Estimate the capacity and duration of short-term memory.

As indicated earlier, many experimental procedures have been used to investigate memory. Some of the earliest demonstrated the existence of a short-term memory with a limited capacity and duration. Techniques Box U describes the *immediate memory span* procedure, which formed part of the earliest intelligence tests developed at the beginning of this century. Miller (1956) in a very influential paper 'The magical number seven, plus or minus two' pointed out that it does not matter what size the 'chunks' are that have to be stored in STM. People can remember seven words just as well as seven digits, although words are longer than digits. If digits or words are grouped into larger chunks even more can be remembered. People who can repeat back very long lists of numbers do it by grouping the numbers together into long mathematical sequences. Their memory span is the normal seven to nine items but the 'items' are twenty digit strings.

TECHNIQUES BOX U

Immediate Memory Span

A list of items (e.g. 7 8 3 4 7 1 0 6) is read aloud and the subject is asked to repeat them back immediately in the correct order. The number of items in the list can be increased on successive trials until the subject starts to make errors in recalling the items. The maximum number of items that subjects can consistently recall in this way is referred to as their immediate memory span, which for adults varies from around seven to nine items. This number is taken as reflecting the capacity of the short-term memory store (STM).

Memory span is concerned with the capacity of short-term memory rather than its duration, since the items have to be repeated back immediately. Other researchers have investigated how long items can be held in STM, as described in Techniques Box V.

Peterson and Peterson interpreted their results as evidence that material in STM is forgotten within a period of six to eighteen seconds. Their view of how forgetting occurs is that STM consists of a trace which gradually decays; this is called the *trace decay theory of forgetting*. Rehearsal, it is argued, prevents forgetting because it keeps replenishing the trace before it decays completely.

SAQ 55
How did Peterson and Peterson prevent rehearsal in their experiment?

An alternative explanation about what causes forgetting is that items get confused with one another. This is called the *interference theory of forgetting* because items in memory start 'interfering' with memory for other items. We will look at this theory in more detail in Section 4.4 when considering interference in long-term memory. But many memory theorists believe that interference occurs in STM as well, especially in an experiment like Peterson and Peterson's in which subjects were given so many trials that they ended up by having to recall literally hundreds of trigrams. The suggestion that all these trigrams might have become confused with each other is supported by the fact that, on the very first trial, subjects could remember the first trigram they heard perfectly well even after counting backwards for 18 seconds. It was only after hearing several trigrams that they began to give incorrect recalls.

TECHNIQUES BOX V

Peterson and Peterson's (1959) Trigram Experiment

Peterson and Peterson wanted to study the rate of forgetting for items that are well within the memory span, so they chose single *trigrams* consisting of letters like XPJ. The trouble is that people can obviously remember a single trigram by repeating it over and over to themselves. In order to prevent rehearsal of the trigrams, subjects were given a task to do in between hearing a trigram and recalling it, known as an *interpolated task*. In this experiment, the interpolated task consisted of asking subjects to count backwards in threes, which it was assumed would prevent them from rehearsing. After periods of either 0,3,6,9,12,15 or 18 seconds counting backwards, a tone was sounded for the subjects to stop counting and try to recall the trigram.

Peterson and Peterson scored subjects' recalls as correct only when letters were reported in the correct order. Figure 4.2 shows the results they obtained. The average percentage recall of trigrams is high after short delays of three or six seconds but falls as the delay period increases. After eighteen seconds of delay, subjects were correctly recalling only 10 per cent of the trigrams.

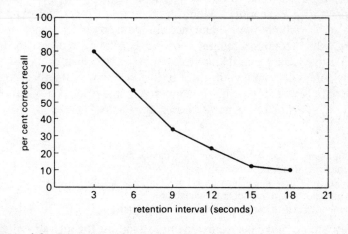

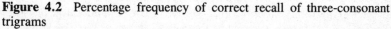

Figure 4.2 Percentage frequency of correct recall of three-consonant trigrams

Key Notes 4.3

1 Memory span measures the number of items which can be repeated back immediately in the correct order, normally about seven items, either single digits or larger 'chunks' like words.

2 The Peterson and Peterson study demonstrated forgetting of trigrams (three consonants) after eighteen seconds of interpolated activity (counting backwards). This has been attributed to decay of the short-term memory trace; an alternative explanation is that forgetting is caused by interference from the many different trigrams to be remembered in the experiment.

3 STM is estimated to have a capacity of five to nine items (immediate memory span) and a duration of six to twelve seconds (Peterson and Peterson).

4.4 LONG-TERM MEMORY

Diagnostic Questions for Section 4.4

1 Distinguish between semantic and episodic memory.
2 What are the advantages of using lists of nonsense syllables for testing memory?
3 Evaluate evidence for the interference theory of forgetting in LTM.

Tulving (1972) introduced a distinction between two types of long-term memory: *episodic memory*, which is memory for personal experiences and episodes which have happened in your own life, and *semantic memory*, which contains general knowledge. One difficulty with this distinction is that most general knowledge must have been discovered by way of a particular episode in your life. For instance, when did my recognition of the Eiffel Tower stop being remembered from episodes of visiting Paris and become part of my general knowledge?

SAQ 56
Are the following examples of episodic or semantic memory?
(a) remembering a telephone number
(b) recalling your first day at primary school
(c) remembering how to do quadratic equations
(d) remembering which cards you have played in a game of cards

Very few studies have been carried out to examine the memory of real life episodes. A notable exception is a study by Brown and Kulik (1977) who asked people to remember what they were doing at the time they heard about John Kennedy's assassination. Typically people had extremely vivid *'flashbulb' memories* of what was happening in their personal life at that moment.

The sheer individuality of these kinds of episodic memories, resulting from everyone's unique experiences, make them very difficult to study experimentally. So, while it is accepted that long-term memory contains all the memories stored in our minds, nearly all the classic experiments on

LTM have concentrated upon memory 'episodes' which operate over minutes or hours rather than months or years. Moreover, studies have tended to be restricted to remembering lists of words which 'the experimenter told me to remember'. In fact, interest in how lists of items are stored in memory stemmed from the earliest experiments in memory by Ebbinghaus (1885), who used himself as his own subject in a long series of experiments (see Techniques Box W).

TECHNIQUES BOX W

Ebbinghaus' Experiments

Ebbinghaus wanted to standardize his experimental investigations as much as possible, so he decided to use *nonsense syllables* as the to-be-remembered materials, 'consonant-vowel-consonant' (CVCs for short) such as WUX, CAZ, JEK, FUP. He rejected words as stimuli because he felt that words might have special meaningful associations which would make some easier to learn than others. Ebbinghaus made up hundreds of CVC lists and read them out loud to himself, over and over again. By varying the number of times he went through a list, or the delay between learning and recalling a list, he was able to study factors which influence learning and forgetting.

When he had reached the stage where he could repeat lists of thirteen CVCs accurately, Ebbinghaus retested himself on the lists after delays varying from twenty minutes to thirty-one days. He tested his memory by seeing how many times he had to go through the lists again in order to relearn them. This is known as the *'savings' method* because it measures the number of trials saved when you relearn something you have already learnt before.

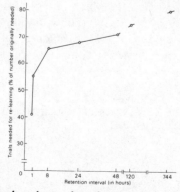

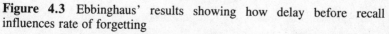

Figure 4.3 Ebbinghaus' results showing how delay before recall influences rate of forgetting

---

Figure 4.3 shows that the longer the delay (*retention interval*) between original learning and testing, the more re-learning trials were required.

Notice that forgetting was very rapid at first, most of it happening in the first hour after learning. After that forgetting slows down; you need scarcely more re-learning trials after two days than you need after eight hours, or even after a month (744 hours = 31 days!).

SAQ 57
Name another experiment which used nonsense syllables.

Another traditional memory paradigm, which was developed to investigate S-R learning in humans, is shown in Techniques Box X.

TECHNIQUES BOX X

Paired Associate Learning

In this procedure subjects have to learn associations between pairs of items; for example, a pair might consist of a nonsense syllable paired with a digit, like NIZ-5. The subject learns to respond with the second part of each pair when he is presented with the first. For example, the experimenter might present NIZ-? and the subject has to say '5'; he has to learn to associate the response 5 to the stimulus NIZ. In paired-associate learning items are not presented in a fixed order. For example, the items NIZ-5 and TOK-3 might be adjacent pairs in one memory test and separated in another trial; however, NIZ and 5 would always be paired with each other, as would TOK and 3.

The paired associate procedure was used in the 1940s and 1950s to investigate the learning and forgetting of S-R links. In particular, it led to the *interference theory of forgetting*, which proposed that forgetting occurs because correct responses get confused with (i.e. interfered with) by competing incorrect responses. Two techniques designed to investigate the effect of interference between competing responses are shown in Techniques Box Y.

SAQ 58
Look back to Techniques Box V. Which kinds of interference (RI or PI) might be operating in the Peterson and Peterson experiment?

Key Notes 4.4

1 Semantic memory refers to all the general knowledge a person has about the world. Episodic memory refers to memory for episodes and personal experiences.
2 Ebbinghaus initiated the search for neutral items like nonsense syllables which would have no special associations, the aim being to study 'pure' memory.

3 The Retroactive Inhibition (RI) and Proactive Inhibition (PI) paradigms demonstrate that both prior learning and later learning may cause interference; the more similar the interfering materials the more confusion there is between items in memory.

TECHNIQUES BOX Y

Retroactive Inhibition and Proactive Inhibition

Subjects learn a list of paired associates denoted an 'A-B' list in which A and B are the generic names for the stimulus items and response items respectively. For example, an A-B list might contain pairs like CIZ-7 and KAX-3, in which the A stimulus items would be CIZ and KAX and the B response items would be 7 and 3. An A-C list refers to a list of paired associates, using the same A items as stimuli, but different C response items. For example, an A-C list might contain items like CIZ-8 and KAX-2, in which CIZ and KAX would still be the A stimulus items as before, but 8 and 2 would be the new C response items. The idea is that, if a subject has to learn both an A-B and an A-C list, the B and C response items will interfere with each other; given the stimulus CIZ, the person does not know whether the B response 7 or the C response 8 is correct, since both have been associated with the A item CIZ as S-R links.

There are two techniques for demonstrating interference: Retroactive Inhibition (RI) and Proactive Inhibition (PI), 'inhibition' because the B and C responses are thought of as inhibiting each other. The difference between the two techniques is that in *retroactive inhibition (RI)* the interfering A-C list has a backwards (retro) interfering effect on the original A-B list. For this reason the A-C list is presented as an interpolated task after the A-B list to see whether learning the A-C pairs effects memory for the A-B pairs.

Retroactive Inhibition (RI)
Learn A-B   Learn A-C   Recall A-B

In *proactive interference* the interfering A-C list has a forwards (pro) interfering effect on the A-B list, so the A-C list is learned before the A-B list to see whether, even when the A-C pairs are learned before the correct responses, they can still cause interference in memory.

Proactive Inhibition (PI)
Learn   A-C   Learn   A-B   Recall   A-B

In general, both RI and PI lead to decreased performance on the recall of the A-B items, as compared with recall performance when there are no interfering lists, indicating that both RI and PI can have a bad effect on memory. This interference effect has been shown to be particularly strong when the response items in the A-B and A-C lists are of the same type or very similar, e.g. NIZ-6 versus NIZ-8. When the new response items in the A-C list are very different, e.g. learning NIZ-6 in the A-B list and NIZ-rabbit in the A-C list, there is much less interference between competing responses.

4.5 COMPARISON BETWEEN STM AND LTM

Diagnostic Questions for Section 4.5

1 List differences between the capacity and duration of STM and LTM.
2 Compare trace decay and interference theories of forgetting.
3 What is the recency effect and what does it imply about short-term memory?
4 Describe experiments which distinguish between visual, acoustic and semantic representations in STM and LTM.
5 Evaluate the relevance of patients with clinical amnesias to theories of memory.

Originally STM and LTM experiments seemed to be clearly distinguished by the procedures used to test them. Immediate memory span or forgetting trigrams after eighteen seconds were obvious cases of STM, while remembering lists of words for half an hour were examples of LTM. This led to a distinction being made between STM and LTM on the basis of storage capacity, time intervals, and type of forgetting. STM can hold only a few items (7 + or − 2) for a few seconds, whereas LTM is supposed to be unlimited in that it contains everything we know; though our capacity for remembering lists of nonsense syllables for even half an hour is actually quite limited!

Traditionally, it has been assumed that forgetting from STM is due to rapid decay over a few seconds unless items are rehearsed (Techniques Box V). Forgetting from LTM is thought to be due to interference from competing responses (Techniques Box Y) which makes it difficult to retrieve the original response. However, this distinction has become somewhat blurred since interference from similar tasks can affect even STM.

Under the influence of the multistore information processing model of memory, in the 1960s attention shifted from separate procedures for STM and LTM to an interest in how short-term and long-term stores might both contribute in different ways to the storage of information. One example was the role of STM and LTM in learning lists of words. Most of the original work on list learning had required subjects to output the items in the same order in which they were presented, known as *serial learning*. This means that all items have to remain in memory for the same length of time since the first items have to be output first and the last items last. In order to study the role of STM in learning, the *free recall* paradigm was invented which allowed subjects to recall the words in a list in any order they wished. It may, of course, seem odd to the layman that this method of 'free' recall was not the obvious way to measure memory in the first place.

TECHNIQUES BOX Z

Free Recall Experiments

The difference between serial learning and free recall is that, in free recall, the lists of words to be learnt are still presented in a predetermined order but the subjects are allowed to recall the items in any order they please: for instance, producing the last items first. In order to show whether items at the beginning or end of a list are more likely to be remembered better, the position of the items in the original presented list (30 items in this case) is plotted along the bottom of a graph, as shown in Figure 4.4. Up the vertical axis are shown the average probabilities of subjects recalling each word correctly depending on its position in the original list.

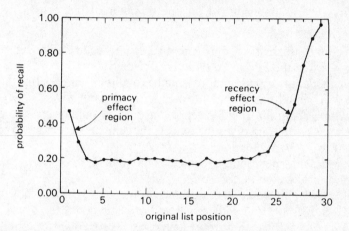

Figure 4.4 Recall for thirty-word lists presented at one second per word (Murdock, 1962).

You will notice that people tend to recall more items which were originally at the beginning and end of the presented list and less items from the middle of the list. This pattern is found very commonly in memory for lists of items and is known as the *serial position effect*.

SAQ 59
In Figure 4.4 it is the percentage of correctly recalled items that is plotted up the vertical axis. It is also possible to plot number of errors up the vertical axis against original item position. Draw a rough graph showing the serial position effect as a relationship between errors and the original position of items in a list which included just five items.

The serial position effect has been reinterpreted as two effects called the primacy effect and the recency effect. The *primacy effect* refers to the better recall of items at the beginning of a list and the *recency effect* refers to the better recall of the last three or four items at the end of the list, i.e.

the items most recently presented. From these results, psychologists have argued that the primacy effect is due to the fact that the first items in the list are more likely to have entered LTM for relatively permanent storage. The recency effect is attributed to STM since the last items in the list will have been the most recent to enter STM. This is based on the assumption that the final items are produced first because they are still in STM. The primacy and recency effects have been considered to be strong evidence for the existence of two separate STM and LTM stores, STM for storing the most recent items in a list and LTM for storing the first few items.

Another basis for distinguishing between STM and LTM is the way in which items are coded. *Coding*, also known as *encoding*, refers to the way in which information is internally represented at various stages in an information processing model. Codes are usually distinguished according to modality, i.e. as being based on one or other of our senses, as listed below.

Visual code: information represented as visual features like size, shape, colour − often thought to be like visual 'images'.
Acoustic code: information represented as auditory features like pitch and loudness, a sound-based code (also called *phonemic code*).
Articulatory code: information represented as it would be spoken; similar to acoustic code but involves the muscle movements necessary to produce sounds (also called *phonological code*).
Motor code: information represented as movements necessary to perform an action (also called *action code*).
Semantic code: information represented as meanings, usually meanings of words; often contrasted with visual and acoustic codes.
Verbal code: information represented as words; can refer either to acoustic features of letters or words (as opposed to a visual code) or to the names of letters and words.

SAQ 60
(a) How might a telephone number you have looked up be coded while you walk across a room to dial it?
(b) What would be the most likely code(s) for a diagram of instructions for assembling a piece of furniture?
(c) If someone was using a visual code, which of the following letters would they be most likely to mistake for one another? T Q Y C B O.
(d) If they were using an acoustic code, which letters would be most likely to be confused?

One common experimental technique for investigating which code is being used is to look at *confusion errors*. The assumption is that, if subjects confuse items, then the codings in which those items are internally represented must have been so similar that the person cannot distinguish between them. Conrad (1964) showed that, even when groups of letters are presented visually and subjects are asked to write them down, people make mistakes based on the sounds of the letters. For instance, when a B was presented there were 102 cases of P errors but only six of F, which is quite like P visually but has a different sound. From this it was deduced that, although the letters had been presented visually, they had been re-coded into an acoustic coding in STM since subjects could not remember whether they had seen B or P.

Another measure of confusability between items is to assume that people find it harder to learn the order of items which are coded in the same way and so are easily confusable.

TECHNIQUES BOX AA

Acoustically and semantically similar words in STM and LTM

Baddeley (1966) asked subjects to learn the order of a list of acoustically similar words (e.g. mad, cap, man), a list of semantically similar words (e.g. huge, big, great) or a list of ordinary unrelated words. When subjects were asked to put the words in each list in the correct order immediately after they had heard them (STM), they made most mistakes with the list of acoustically similar words. When they reordered the words after twenty minutes (LTM), it was the list of semantically similar words that proved most difficult. This was interpreted as showing that an acoustic coding is used in STM, making it difficult to sort out the similar sounding words. In LTM subjects stored the words semantically and so could not distinguish between words like huge and great, which would have been coded in LTM as having the same meanings.

Results from experiments like Conrad's and Baddeley's have been quoted as evidence that there must be separate STM and LTM stores in which items are coded in different ways: acoustic coding in STM and semantic coding in LTM.

Finally, there is another quite different kind of evidence for a distinction between STM and LTM which has come from studying patients suffering from *amnesia* (loss of memory). Various types of brain damage can be shown to affect STM and LTM in different ways, which suggests that they must be separate systems.

TECHNIQUES BOX BB

Amnesia and Memory

One example of *traumatic amnesia* ('trauma' here means 'caused by injury') is the effect of a blow on the head. When people come round they may have forgotten (i.e. have permanent amnesia) for the few moments before the accident (STM) but retain memory of everything that happened prior to that point (LTM). *(continued on p. 88)*

Another cause of permanent amnesia is the *Korsakov syndrome* which results from severe alcohol poisoning. Patients with Korsakov syndrome forget all new material within seconds of receiving it; for instance they fail to recognize their doctor even after hundreds of visits. Their LTM for events before their illness seems unaffected − they can recall events in their childhood, and people and places they used to know. Their immediate memory spans (STM) are also unimpaired. What seems to be impaired is the transfer of material from STM to LTM, which is, of course, all important for learning.

A very few patients have been identified with the opposite amnesia: a fully functioning LTM but a very short memory span and a recency effect of only one item. Here the transfer from STM to LTM is proceeding normally but there may not be much in STM at any one time to transfer. Interestingly, one of these patients, KF, had difficulties in reading and occasionally in speaking, implying that STM is involved in holding together words in a sentence. Nevertheless, a case like this does seem to show that material can be directly stored in LTM without being held for long in STM.

Key Notes 4.5

1 STM is considered to have a limited capacity of anything from the three or four most recent items in a list (recency effect) to five to nine items (immediate memory span). If rehearsal is prevented, it is estimated that items will decay after a few seconds. Storage and duration of knowledge in LTM is in principle unlimited; but memories cannot always be retrieved.

2 The traditional theory of forgetting is that STM is susceptible to rapid decay while forgetting in LTM is caused by interference from competing responses. However, there is evidence that STM tasks can also be affected by interference.

3 The recency effect refers to the fact that in free recall the last few items in a list are recalled better than the rest of the list. This is generally taken as evidence that these items are stored in STM. The primacy effect is attributed to the storage of the first few items in LTM.

4 The main types of coding are visual, acoustic and semantic codes. Experiments have demonstrated that acoustic confusions occur in STM and semantic confusions in LTM, indicating that items are represented as acoustic codes in STM and semantic codes in LTM.

5 Amnesia patients who suffer differential deficits for STM and LTM can throw light on the functions of different components of memory.

4.6 WORKING MEMORY AND LEVELS OF PROCESSING

Diagnostic Questions for Section 4.6

1 Contrast the concept of working memory with earlier models of short-term memory.
2 Describe experimental techniques to investigate subsystems within working memory.
3 What is the basic principle of the levels of processing theory?
4 What is the major difficulty of studying how people use their memories?

The findings reported in the last section imply that there are physiological and psychological differences between two separate stores, STM responsible for brief storage of a few items and LTM for long-term storage of everything we know. However, it might be more reasonable to think that people use all available memory systems to store items in the most appropriate way to be recalled as required. The tendency in the 1970s and 1980s has been to move away from the notion of separate stores and instead to concentrate on the functions of various memory systems.

For instance, if you stop thinking of STM simply as a temporary store and consider instead the functions such a temporary system might serve, a very different model of memory emerges. Looked at in this way, STM is where active processing goes on, for instance rehearsing items either to retain them in STM or to commit them to LTM. Instead of being a passive store, STM becomes the place where decisions are made about how to tackle memory problems, a concept captured by the term working memory.

Baddeley (1981) and his colleagues have developed a theory of *working memory (WM)* which attempts to specify which components of a short-term memory system might be involved in various tasks (see Techniques Box CC on p.90).

The greatest difficulty has arisen in investigating the central executive processor. The problem is that its role is very wide, including deciding on strategies for allocating attention to different tasks, retrieving necessary information from LTM, and preparing appropriate responses.

SAQ 61
How does this notion of working memory fit in with Kahneman's theory of attention described in Section 2.5 of the Attention Module?

Baddeley's model captures the fact that we use our memories to do things, probably more frequently than to repeat back facts, at least after we have left school. By implication it also locates the site of consciousness in WM in that it is responsible for selecting inputs and accessing LTM; planning strategies for solving problems and outputting appropriate responses.

TECHNIQUES BOX CC

Concurrent tasks in WM

One of Baddeley's methodologies has been to occupy STM with a concurrent task while people are carrying out tasks which are thought to involve WM, for example, doing mental arithmetic or solving puzzles. The rationale is that, if one task interferes with the other, then they must be using the same component of memory; if not, they are using different components. Baddeley found that people can perform quite well on problems even while they are asked to remember three or more digits at the same time. Try, for instance, remembering the digits 2478 (put your hand over them) and at the same time adding 45 and 22. Baddeley interpreted these results as showing that WM includes both an *articulatory loop*, in which three or four items can be rehearsed, and a *central executive processor*. As long as the number of items in a traditional STM memory task can be handled by the articulatory loop, the central processor is available for other tasks. However, if the number of items is too much for the loop, they begin to encroach on the capacity of the central processor.

Although Baddeley's approach proposes a more dynamic function for working memory, his research was still carried out within the framework of the multistore model of memory, dividing the original short-term store into subsystems with different functions like the articulatory loop and the central executive.

A rather more radical approach is to suggest that there are no separate stores for STM and LTM. Instead the strength of a memory depends on how deeply material is processed in the first place. This *levels of processing* approach (Craik and Lockheart, 1972) suggests that memory is a by-product of perceptual processing rather than a series of stores. Craik and Lockheart allow for recirculation of items in STM (which they call *primary memory*) by repeating, say, a telephone number over and over again to keep it in the forefront of attention; but once rehearsal ceases the item immediately disappears. This would presumably be the equivalent of Baddeley's articulatory loop.

All material which is to be retained for longer periods in LTM (which they call *secondary memory*) will need to be processed at some level. The shallower the level of processing the more transitory will be the memory; deeper processing will lead to longer lasting memories. This model captures the intuitive distinction between material that we try to learn thoroughly as opposed to facts we might mug up to pass an exam! In real life, of course, everybody makes their own selection of what to process more or less deeply.

Craik and his colleagues devised an ingenious incidental learning procedure for getting people to process items at different levels, the point being that, if people realized that their memories were going to be tested, there would be no way of preventing them from processing all the items in the best possible way to remember them (see Techniques Box DD).

TECHNIQUES BOX DD

Levels of Processing Experiments: Incidental Learning Procedure

In order to control the level at which subjects processed items, Craik and Tulving (1975) told their subjects that the experiment was testing perception and speed of reaction. A question was presented and then a word; subjects had to indicate 'yes' or 'no' to the question about the word as quickly as possible. The questions were designed to manipulate the kind of coding of the words subjects had to engage in. The shallowest physical level of coding asked 'Is the word in capital letters?'; the next level of phonemic coding asked 'Does the word rhyme with able?' and the deepest level of semantic coding asked 'Would the word fit the sentence 'The man sat on the ?' followed by a word like 'chair' (yes) or 'tree' (no).

The experimenters were not interested in subjects' reaction times but afterwards unexpectedly gave them a *recognition test*. This means that, instead of recalling the words, subjects were given a long list of words and had to pick out those which they recognized as having seen before. Craik and Tulving found that the deeper the processing level, the more words were recognized correctly; subjects recognized more words when they had had to think whether the meanings fitted a sentence than those words which they had only had to categorize as being in upper case capitals (TABLE) or lower case (chair).

SAQ 62
Indicate whether the following types of processing are shallow or deep,
(a) deciding whether words contain the letter E,
(b) rating words as pleasant or unpleasant.

Many other experiments have confirmed this relationship between depth of processing and retention, regardless of whether subjects have been warned that they will have to recall the words (*intentional learning*) or not (*incidental learning*). An important implication is that memory is not an all-or-nothing affair but depends on how we process inputs. However, the levels of processing explanation turned out to be less simple than at first appeared.

SAQ 63
Suppose that the incidental memory test, instead of testing recognition of words, had required subjects to say whether the words they had seen had been in upper case CAPITAL LETTERS or in ordinary lower case letters. Which group of subjects in the Craik and Tulving experiment would you expect to do best?

The fact that people are more likely to remember cues which they have concentrated on may seem patently obvious. However, such a result challenges the notion that there are stages of processing, starting with shallow processing of physical features like letter case, and only then progressing to phonemic (rhymes) and eventually semantic coding of meanings.

SAQ 64
Which stages in the multistore model of memory in Section 4.1 would these three stages of processing be expected to occur?

Processing conceived as a flow of information through a series of stages has two implications. First, semantic processing should always take more time than shallow physical processing. Second, semantic processing should always be better than shallower processing. However, experiments (Morris, Bransford and Franks, 1977) have shown that carrying out a semantic analysis does not necessarily mean that 'shallower' information like rhymes has also been noted.

As a result of these difficulties, Craik and Tulving abandoned a strict processing stage model in favour of the plausible notion that people select the type of processing most suitable for their needs, for instance, skim reading an article for meaning as opposed to a careful analysis of its physical characteristics for layout on a magazine page.

The problem is that, as the levels of processing model became more flexible, it also became more difficult to test. In the basic experimental procedure tasks were devised to control subjects' processing of inputs, which could later be tested to see what they had learnt incidentally. But, of course, people employ their own strategies for processing inputs from the environment, depending on what they need for a particular purpose.

Key Notes 4.6

1 Baddeley's theory of working memory (WM) concentrates on the functions of short-term memory systems as opposed to a limited capacity STM for storing a few items for a few seconds.

2 Subjects are given concurrent tasks which are thought to employ different components of WM, in order to see whether this affects performance on other tasks.

3 The levels of processing approach, developed by Craik and Lockheart, suggests that memory is a by-product of the depth of processing of inputs; the deeper the processing the better the retention.

4 Both working memory and levels of processing assume that people have flexibility in selecting what to attend to and how to learn; but this flexibility makes it more difficult to control what subjects are processing in psychological experiments.

4.7 STRATEGIES FOR ORGANIZING MEMORY

Diagnostic Questions for Section 4.7

1 What were the main features of Bartlett's theory of memory?
2 Describe the advantages and disadvantages of Bartlett's approach.
3 Evaluate experimental evidence for organization in memory.
4 What are the implications of active models of memory?

In the previous section we have been moving away from the concept of an information processing model, in which information passively flows from one memory store to another, towards the idea of an active central executive which makes decisions about analysing input and deciding what learning strategies are appropriate.

Paradoxically perhaps, this 'new' approach stems from a tradition in memory research almost as early as Ebbinghaus. In 1932 Bartlett published an influential book *Remembering* in which he stressed that memory is not a passive playback of recorded material. Instead we analyse only certain aspects of our environment in the first place and use these cues to reconstruct events. Turn over to p.94 and read Bartlett's famous story in Techniques Box EE.

Bartlett drew attention to the importance of concepts and expectancies, which he called *schemas*, which affect not only what we see but also what we remember. These schemas guide our perceptions and memories and in turn are altered and adapted to incorporate new information.

SAQ 65
Name a model of perception in the Perception Module which is based on similar ideas.

If you have now written down your recall of the War of the Ghosts, compare it with the original. Having tested people at varying intervals from fifteen minutes to ten years after, Bartlett attributed characteristic errors to the processes by which the story was assimilated to people's own schemas. In particular, people omitted details and introduced rationalizations in order to 'reconstruct' the story to make more sense in their own terms. This is what Bartlett meant when he referred to *reconstructive memory*. While Bartlett's analysis undoubtedly squares with our intuitions about how we remember, the main difficulty is how to record errors in a precise and standard form so as to compare one person with another or predict that some passages would lead to particular types of errors more than another.

It is interesting to note that during the period from the 1940s to the 1960s, Bartlett's studies of memory were mostly forgotten while the types of STM and LTM experiments described in Sections 4.3, 4.4 and 4.5 were dominating memory research. It is only in the 1970s and 1980s that psychologists who support a more active approach to perception, attention, learning and memory have paid tribute to Bartlett's ideas, while admitting the difficulties of testing them precisely.

TECHNIQUES BOX EE

War of the Ghosts

Read the following story and five minutes later write down what you can remember. Meanwhile turn back to p.93.

One night two young men from Egulac went down to the river to hunt seals, and while they were there it became foggy and calm. Then they heard war-cries and they thought, 'Maybe this is a war-party.' They escaped to the shore and hid behind a log. Now canoes came up and they heard the noise of paddles and saw one canoe coming up to them. There were five men in the canoe and they said, 'What do you think? We wish to take you along. We are going up the river to make war on the people.'

One of the young men said, 'I have no arrows.' 'Arrows are in the canoe,' they said. 'I will not go. I might be killed. My relatives do not know where I have gone. But you,' he said, turning to the other, 'may go with them.' So one of the young men went, but the other returned home. And the warriors went on up the river to a town on the other side of Kalama. The people came down to the water and they began to fight and many were killed. But presently the young man heard one of the warriors say 'Quick, let us go home: that Indian has been hit.' Now he thought, 'Oh, they are ghosts.' He did not feel sick, but they said he had been shot.

So the canoes went back to Egulac, and the young man went ashore to his house and made a fire. And he told everybody and said, 'Behold, I accompanied the ghosts, and we went to fight. Many of our fellows were killed. They said I was hit but I did not feel sick.'

He told it all and then became quiet. When the sun rose he fell down. Something black came out of his mouth. His face became contorted. The people jumped and cried. He was dead.

Bartlett (1932)

SAQ 66
Taking Bartlett and Ebbinghaus as extreme examples of two psychological traditions, tick the following to indicate the advantages (✓) or disadvantages (x) of each approach.

	Ebbinghaus	Bartlett
Easy to measure performance		
Real-life materials		
Allows for flexibility		
Examines the precise limits of memory		

During the 1950s and 1960s there was one line of research which looked at people's memory strategies. An influential book, by Miller, Galanter and Pribram (1960), *Plans and the Structure of Behaviour*, drew attention to the obvious fact that subjects are always on the look-out for ways of translating even nonsense syllables and digits into meaningful combinations (or chunks) that make them easier to remember. The trouble with classic learning experiments was that there was no way of estimating the effects of these learning strategies. The advent of the free recall method described in Techniques Box Z allowed the possibility of deducing people's strategies from the order in which they chose to output the items. If groups of items come out in 'clusters', it is reasonable to assume that the subject had organized these items together in order to learn the list.

TECHNIQUES BOX FF

Free Recall Experiments on Organization

In a study by Bousfield (1953) subjects were given a list of sixty items to learn, which contained fifteen names of animals, fifteen names of people, fifteen professions and fifteen vegetables, all mixed up together. Subjects were asked to recall the words in any order they liked. Despite the fact that the categories had all been jumbled up together originally, subjects tended to remember them in clusters of words all belonging to the same category. For instance, once they had recalled, say, 'dog', then other animals were likely to follow: 'cat', 'mouse', 'rat', 'horse', 'donkey'. Bousfield concluded that such category clusters are indicative of semantic organization in memory.

Mandler (1967) demonstrated a similar effect by giving subjects packs of word cards which they had to sort out into their own categories. When subjects were later asked to recall as many of the words as possible, Mandler found that subjects clustered the words they recalled according to the categories they had used for sorting.

Despite the fact that the approaches to memory described in this section emphasize the importance of the memorizer's intentions and strategies, in general, memory research has concentrated on memory for specific materials which have been learnt in the (usually very recent) past. Nothing has been said about memory of how to do things, of social conventions, or how we remember, or quite often forget, things we intend to do in the future. To say that someone is forgetful is just as often to mean that they forget to do things as that they have forgotten something they have learned in the past.

An interesting book you might like to read is Neisser's *Everyday memory observed: Remembering in natural contexts*, which rounds up some of the very few experiments done on less conventional aspects of memory.

Finally, what is the current status of the multistore model of memory described in Section 4.1? There has undoubtedly been a move away from regarding STM as primarily a passive limited capacity store for retaining items over a short interval. Instead, STM is thought of as a working memory, possibly with 'slave' systems like articulatory loops for rehearsing items temporarily. Emphasis has shifted from a selective filter, which automatically reduces processing overload, towards an active central processor, which decides at what level to process input, accesses knowledge from LTM and prepares items for output. This applies whether input is to be remembered for a few seconds (traditional STM), half an hour (traditional LTM) or permanently. This model has obvious affinities with Kahneman's allocation model of attention (see Section 2.5 of the Attention Module) and in general allows for the influence of top-down schemas based on experiences and expectations stored in long-term memory.

Most psychologists still accept the general proposition that humans are information processors. The difference is that it is recognized that there are far more links between all parts of the system, involving top-down as well as bottom-up processing. This gives LTM a much more important role as the repository of all stored knowledge rather than a place where soon-to-be-forgotten lists of items are stored for half an hour. The question of how general knowledge is represented in LTM will be covered in another volume of the *Open Guides to Psychology*.

Key Notes 4.7

1 Bartlett emphasized the reconstructive nature of memory, pointing out that memories are not exact copies of events but depend on people's schemas representing past experiences and expectations, essentially a top-down theory.

2 Bartlett used real life materials and identified many intuitively plausible characteristics of memory and forgetting. Since these are difficult to measure, Bartlett's work has tended to inspire later researchers rather than to produce any definite results.

3 One important technique has been to study clustering of items in free recall as a measure of subjects' organizational strategies.

4 The shift towards a more active model of the human processor has led to STM and LTM no longer being regarded as passive stores, but rather as a central processing executive (WM) and a repository of knowledge (LTM), which interact with each other and the perceptual system to react appropriately to the demands of the environment.

READING GUIDE

General Reading

GREGG, V. (1975), *Human Memory*, London, Methuen.
BADDELEY, A. D. (1976), *The Psychology of Memory*, London, Harper

…*ring in Natural*

…Unit 10.
…13, 15.

…5.7, 5.8.

5

Methodology Notes

The aim of the first three sections of these notes is to give you a short outline of the purpose of experiments in psychology. These brief notes may seem rather obscure the first time you read them but in the Introduction you are recommended to read them through again after each module. After reading descriptions of more and more experiments, experimental designs and the kinds of conclusions psychologists draw from them should become more understandable. Sections 5.4 to 5.7 of these notes give you an overview of the methods used in each major topic area, and these should be read immediately after the appropriate module.

Recommended further reading about the design of experiments can be found in D303, Units 5, 12, Section 2. Experimental design and statistical methods for analysing the significance of experimental findings is dealt with in another volume in this series, *Learning to Use Statistical Tests in Psychology: A Student's Guide*, by Judith Greene and Manuela D'Oliveira, published by the Open University Press, Milton Keynes.

5.1 EXPERIMENTS IN PSYCHOLOGY

Psychologists studying basic cognitive processes have been concerned with demonstrating the mechanisms which account for how people see, hear, attend, learn and memorize. The assumption is that these mechanisms are universal to all human beings. Even when past experiences are emphasized as being important for perception and learning, researchers are interested in how these experiences affect responses in general rather than in the quality and content of people's individual experiences.

Since these basic mechanisms consist of internal processes, how do psychologists manage to externalize these processes in a form that can be measured? Secondly, how do psychologists set about investigating what causes people to see things; how and why they attend to certain things and not to others; what makes it easier to learn some things rather than others; what happens to the memories stored inside our heads?

One obvious answer might be, why not ask people? But one thing that this book should have made absolutely clear is that we are unaware of most of these processes. We just seem to see things or find we are attending to something; ideas pop into our heads. Even when we are trying to concentrate on learning something, we are unable to explain how we actually succeed. We can report on what we see, write down what we have learned, but the actual processing is not available to conscious awareness. This is, of course, the main argument against relying on introspective reports.

For this reason, nearly all the research reported in this book uses indirect evidence. The basic *experimental method* is to vary the stimulus input and/or verbal instructions to subjects and record any changes in behaviour (which may include verbal outputs). Take, for example, the experiment described in Techniques Box F in Section 1.8 of the Perception Module. The fact that the 'taboo' words had to be exposed for longer periods before people could report them was interpreted as demonstrating that conscious perceptions can be affected by unconscious anxiety aroused by threatening words. This assumes that verbal reports are an accurate measure of conscious recognition; although, in fact, people might have recognized the words but have been reluctant to report them.

Of course, psychologists don't select at random which inputs to present to the people acting as subjects in an experiment and what aspects of their behaviour to record. Researchers have some theoretical model about psychological processes which suggests a hypothesis about how people might react. In this case Bruner and Postman were testing the hypothesis that people can be unconsciously influenced by emotional reactions.

5.2 EXPERIMENTAL DESIGN

Deciding what kinds of inputs to vary and which aspects of subjects' behaviour to measure is known as *experimental design*. The terminology used defines the inputs as *independent variables* because it is the experimenter who 'independently' decides in what way inputs will 'vary', e.g. presenting threatening or neutral words. The resulting behaviour of the subject is defined as the *dependent variable* because it is 'dependent' on the independent variable, e.g. taking longer to report one type of word than another. The experimenter, on the basis of his or her hypothesis about the causes of behaviour, makes a prediction about the relationship between the independent variable (the input) and the dependent variable (the subject's behaviour). An example would be classical conditioning in which the independent variable is the pairing of the bell and the food and the predicted dependent variable is the dog's response of salivating to the bell alone.

In order to understand the results of experiments, it is essential to grasp what the independent and dependent variables are and how they are varied and measured in each experiment.

SAQ 67
In Bruner and Postman's experiment (Techniques Box F), what was the independent variable (what did the experimenters vary?); the dependent variable (which aspect of people's behaviour was measured?); and what was the predicted relationship between the independent and the dependent variable?

This example points to the need to have two conditions which can be compared. If Bruner and Postman had given their subjects nothing but taboo words and recorded exposure times for recognizing them, how could they have known whether these times — say, half a second — were especially long due to unconscious anxiety? To discover this, they needed to compare these exposure times with the times taken to recognize neutral words. If the exposure times for taboo words were significantly longer than the times for neutral words, then they could conclude that the emotional words were having some extra effect on people's reports.

The neutral words are known as a *control condition* because they provide a 'baseline' against which the experimental condition (the taboo words) can be compared. You will notice that most psychological experiments compare two or more conditions. An example in Section 2.2 of the Attention Module is Broadbent's experiment (Techniques Box G), where subjects were instructed to report the inputs either 'ear by ear' or 'pair by pair' and the number of items correctly recalled under the two conditions was compared. An example in Section 4.6 of the Memory Module is Baddeley's experimental methodology (Techniques Box CC), where he compared people's ability to solve problems like mental arithmetic, both normally and while they had to remember four digits during the task. If he had not included the control condition of normal problem solving, he would not have been able to tell whether people's performance in the experimental condition (having to remember digits) was worse or the same as their normal performance.

5.3 MEASURES OF BEHAVIOUR

You have probably noticed the variety of experimental designs shown in the Techniques Boxes. Some of these are particular to a topic, like the conditioning techniques in the Learning Module; other experimental procedures are used more generally and have become known as *experimental paradigms*.

Among these are a surprisingly short list of techniques for measuring the behaviour of subjects in experiments, i.e. the dependent variable. The main methods are listed below:

1 *Introspective reports* (telling the experimenter what the subject sees, feels or thinks).

2 *Reaction times* (time taken to produce a response).
3 *Learning trials* (number of trials needed to learn or relearn something).
4 *Correct responses* (number of correct responses, correct recall or recognition of items).
5 *Errors* (number of errors made on a task).
6 *Strength of responses* (amount of a response, e.g. saliva).
7 *Frequency of responses* (how often a response occurs, e.g. pecks).
8 Recording *electro-chemical activity* of brain cells (e.g. whether a cell reacts to a particular type of stimulus input).
9 *'Natural'* experiments (e.g. investigating the abilities of clinical patients).

SAQ 68
Which of all these measures are most suitable for measuring human behaviour, animal behaviour, or both?

These measures constitute a battery of techniques which psychologists can use to test their predictions about human behaviour. In the next four sections, we will describe the major methods used in the different modules.

5.4 METHODS FOR STUDYING PERCEPTION

The main methodology for studying human perception has been to vary inputs to the senses, as the independent variable, to see what effect this has on the dependent variable of the verbal reports people give about what they see or hear. These perceptual demonstrations rely on introspective reports to carefully controlled inputs so that conclusions can be drawn about the existence of mechanisms for detecting changes in sensory stimulation (Techniques Box B) and organization of figures against background (Techniques Box C). Demonstrations of perceptual illusions and interpretations of ambiguous figures also fall into this category (Techniques Box D).

When it is a question of investigating the perceptual mechanisms of organisms which can't talk about what they see, other methods have to be used. With animals it is possible to record the activity of nerve cells (Techniques Box A). With newborn infants it is necessary to employ indirect measures of their perceptions, such as how long they fixate their gaze on an object (Techniques Box E).

So far we have been talking about perceptions which can be demonstrated in various ways. What about models which attempt to specify the unconscious bottom-up and top-down processing which results in the perception and recognition of objects? One line of research manipulates the presentation of meaningful inputs at a level below the conscious awareness of subjects, as the independent variable, and measures any effects on the times taken to respond, as the dependent variable (Techniques Box F). This is taken as showing that the meanings of inputs can have an unconscious top-down influence on reported perceptions.

5.5 METHODS FOR STUDYING ATTENTION

By far the most common method for externalizing the internal mental processes underlying attention is the *divided attention paradigm*, usually involving presenting different inputs through headphones to each ear. The rationale is that the ears act as two separate channels, which makes it possible to examine under what conditions people attend to one or other ear. The experimenter can vary inputs to the ears and/or instructions to the subject, as the independent variable, to see what effect this has on the dependent variable of the subjects' verbal reports, which are used as a measure of conscious attention.

In Broadbent's split-span procedure (Techniques Box G), the independent variable was the instructions to recall ear-by-ear or pair-by-pair to see how this affected the dependent variable of how many digits subjects could recall. In the shadowing procedure (Techniques Box H), the subject's attention is directed to shadowing a message in the attended ear while inputs to the unattended ear can be varied to see what people notice. Another version of the shadowing technique is to vary messages to the unattended ear to see whether they affect verbal reports of the attended message, even though subjects may not be consciously aware of the unattended inputs (Techniques Box I).

Later research, under the influence of Kahneman's theory, investigated people's ability to divide their attention between more than one thing at a time. In dual task experiments, the independent variables are the two tasks and the dependent variable is people's performance on the tasks. These still count as divided attention experiments but, rather than concentrating on competing auditory inputs to the ears, the tasks used different modalities and so provided evidence for multichannel processing (Techniques Box J).

In Neisser's visual search experiment to test pre-attentional parallel processing, he varied the number of targets subjects had to search for, as the independent variable, to see whether this affected the dependent variable of reaction times to locate the targets (Techniques Box K).

5.6 METHODS FOR STUDYING LEARNING

The methods used in classical behaviourism are rather different from those discussed so far. For one thing, nearly all the research was done using animals. Rightly or wrongly, depending on your point of view, this allowed experimenters to subject them to starvation and shocks, and to confine them in boxes and mazes. Another factor was that, whereas the experiments in the Attention Module were designed to decide between competing models of selective attention, researchers into learning wanted to demonstrate the basic laws of conditioning. Perhaps it was because they were dealing with animals that theories of learning seemed more 'universal' and immutable than models of human information processing. Finally, the ethos of behaviourism was to rule out introspective verbal reports, another obvious advantage of using non-talking animals.

The basic method in conditioning experiments is to vary inputs to the animal including stimuli and reinforcements, as the independent variables, and to measure as the dependent variable the occurrence of learned responses. Measures of learning include the strength or amount of responses, like salivating (Techniques Box L); speed of responses, like pulling a string to get out of a box (Techniques Box M) or time to run a maze; frequency of responses, like pecks or pressing a lever (Techniques Boxes N, P and Q); correctness of responses, as in the shaping procedure (Techniques Box O), reduction of errors (Techniques Box R) or avoidance of a response (Techniques Box S).

5.7 METHODS FOR STUDYING MEMORY

Most experiments in memory research are designed to test predictions about how human memory works. While many of the models were developed within the multistore information processing framework, the models themselves are many and various, each tending to focus on particular aspects of one stage in the memory process.

The earliest experiments by Ebbinghaus (Techniques Box W) initiated learning and recall of lists of items, like nonsense syllables, as the dominant experimental paradigm in memory research. In general, whatever the types of material to be learnt, the most common measures of the dependent variable of memory performance are number of items recalled, items recognized and/or errors made.

In Sperling's technique for studying sensory memory, the same methods were used as for studying perception or attention, i.e. varying inputs and instructions (cues) to see the effect on subjects' reports (Techniques Box T); this is not surprising as SM is equivalent to the registration of sensory information before it is selected for further processing.

The capacity (span) of STM was measured by varying the number of items to be repeated back (Techniques Box U) and its duration by varying delays before recall (Techniques Box V). Another more indirect method for estimating the capacity of STM is the number of recent items remembered from the end of a list in free recall, the recency effect (Techniques Box Z). In order to test the interference theory of forgetting, different kinds of paired-associate lists were varied, as the independent variable, to test whether they have a damaging effect on subjects' recalls, as compared with a control condition with no interfering lists (Techniques Boxes X and Y).

Experiments investigating the internal codings used to represent memories in STM and LTM often depend on indirect evidence from confusion errors. The assumption is that, if subjects confuse items which are similar on some modality dimension, e.g. they look alike, sound alike or have the same meaning, it can be deduced that people's codings are based on that modality and so are responsible for the confusion (Techniques Box AA).

Methods for investigating memory systems include Baddeley's technique of presenting concurrent tasks, on the basis that, since tasks which use the same system should interfere with each other, tasks which can be done simultaneously must be using separate subsystems (Techniques Box CC). Notice this is the same methodology as the dual task experiments (Techniques Box J in Section 2.5 of the Attention Module), which were interpreted as evidence in favour of separate processing systems for each modality.

Tests of the levels of processing approach involved asking people to process items in different ways, as the independent variable, testing effects on memory by an incidental learning procedure in which subjects were faced with an unexpected recognition test (Techniques Box DD). Research into people's strategies, when they know they have to learn something, attempted to formalize Bartlett's intuitive interpretations of people's errors (Techniques Box EE) by analysing the order in which people recall clusters of items as the dependent variable (Techniques Box FF).

A final indication of the variety of methods used in memory research is the conclusions drawn from the different kinds of memory deficits experienced by clinical patients who suffer from loss of memory, i.e. amnesias (Techniques Box BB).

5.8 SOME PROBLEMS

There is no doubt that the main methodology for studying basic cognitive processes has been the use of experiments to test predictions derived from theoretical models. If the predictions are upheld by the findings of experiments, the model gains support; if an experiment results in contradictory findings, the model should be rejected in favour of another theory.

However, there are certain things you should bear in mind:

1 You may have noticed that virtually all experiments appear to support the experimenter's model. One reason for this is that psychologists do not usually publish the results of experiments which 'failed' to find the expected results although, of course, these may have led them to modify their theory.
2 Nearly all experiments use artificial materials and situations which do not mirror the real life events they are trying to explain. How often in real life do we peer down a tachistoscope at words flashed for a fraction of a second; or count backwards in threes while trying to remember a nonsense syllable? In view of the complex conclusions about people's mental abilities based on such experiments, some psychologists feel that more attention ought to be paid to what subjects think they are doing, even at the risk of asking them.
3 The vast majority of psychology experiments have been carried out by university researchers using their 18-21 year old students. Can we be sure that members of the general population would react in the same way?
4 A related danger is that people devise special strategies to produce what they think the experimenter wants, rather than attending or learning normally; this is known as the *demand characteristics* of the experimental situation itself, which may be affecting subjects' behaviour much more than the experimenter realizes.

5.9 A HISTORICAL NOTE

You may have noticed that sometimes research in an area seems to go off on another tack, without necessarily proving that previous models where actually 'wrong'. Examples are the reaction against early introspective methods by the experimental Black Box ethos of behaviourism; the emergence of the information processing model in the 1950s which gave rise to models of perception, attention, sensory memory, STM and LTM as boxes representing stage posts in a one-way bottom-up flow of information; the shift towards people's top-down strategies using 'schemas', based on past experiences, and making decisions about how to divide their attention to deal with problems in their environment. Earlier psychologists who had fallen from favour, like Bartlett and Tolman, were now quoted as forerunners of this interest in mental representations, the new 'cognitive' approach.

You should bear all this in mind when you look at the Historical Chart and Overview of Models. But remember that, despite our somewhat disparaging remarks about experimental methods, there have been a lot of ingenious and well-designed experiments which have illuminated hitherto unknown psychological processes. When reading about experiments you should be able to think critically about their aims, methods and results. Psychology is still a developing science, with many avenues to follow to understand the full complexities of human behaviour.

Historical Chart

Overview of Models

Answers to SAQs

Historical Chart

Dates	Perception	Attention	Learning	Memory
1880	Wundt and the Psychophysicists		Pavlov Thorndike	Ebbinghaus Immediate memory span
1920	Gestalt school		Watson (Black Box)	
1930			Tolman Skinner	Bartlett
1940			Hull	
1950	Perceptual defence experiments	Broadbent's information processing model		Interference theory of forgetting (LTM) Peterson (STM)
1960	Hubel and Wiesel Pandemonium Neisser	Treisman's model Deutsch/Norman model Neisser	'Biological' approach to conditioning	Sperling (SM) Multistore model
1970		Kahneman's model Dual task experiments		Levels of processing Working memory
1980				

Overview of Models

1920s   Classic Behaviourism

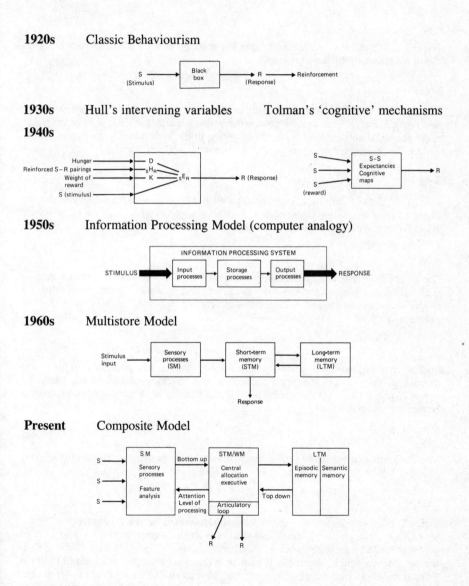

1930s   Hull's intervening variables   Tolman's 'cognitive' mechanisms
1940s

1950s   Information Processing Model (computer analogy)

1960s   Multistore Model

Present   Composite Model

Answers to SAQs

SAQ 1

The sense organs are eyes for vision, ears for hearing, skin for touch, taste buds in the mouth for taste and the nose for smell.

SAQ 2

The increased noise would be more likely to be noticed in the 'quieter' atmosphere of the piano recital. But, of course, the type of noise is also important; a loud chord on the piano might not be so noticeable as 'softer' whispering in the audience. The psychophysicists ignored the 'meanings' of inputs in their search for 'pure' sensations.

SAQ 3

In Figure 1.5 the 4 is more effectively concealed in (i) because we are likely to see the whole diagram as a single figure with a continuous contour, whereas in (ii) the contours of the 4 are quite distinct from the other lines and so the 4 stands out as a figure on its own.

SAQ 4

The psychophysicists and the Gestalt psychologists differed because the former investigated isolated sensations and the latter the perception of whole figures. Both relied on people's verbal reports and believed that perception was the result of physiological mechanisms in the visual system.

SAQ 5

(a) The square because it is in front of the circle (known as interposition); (b) the pencil because we know that pencils are smaller than vans, therefore to look so big it must be nearer (familiar size); (c) the square because the lines make it look as if the triangle is further away (perspective).

SAQ 6

The illusion that the top line is further away depends on the perspective cue of railway lines disappearing into the distance, as in Figure 1.7 (c).

SAQ 7

Figure 1.7 (c) provides texture cues to distance gradients in the visual field received by the retina. One could also imagine that physical cues about whether one object is in front of the other could be picked up by the retina, perhaps according to the Gestalt law of continuation which would indicate that the square with an uninterrupted contour is a figure in front of the circle with a broken contour. But what about (b)? How could the nerve cells in the retina, which transmit sensory information about the physical characteristics of the visual field, 'know' that pencils are smaller than vans?

SAQ 8

The knowledge that a pencil is usually smaller than a van is based on our previous experience of these objects, an example of prior knowledge influencing perception in a top-down direction.

SAQ 9

Hallucinations or dreaming are examples of perceptions which are entirely based on the mental activity going on inside our minds, without any bottom-up retinal input.

SAQ 10

Ambiguous figures have one sensory input but several possible perceptions; perceptual constancies have several sensory inputs (e.g. as we move away from an object) which result in one perception (of an object with a constant size).

SAQ 11

Bottom-up processing is concerned with the transmission of basic sensory information through the visual system and so is more likely to be accounted for by inborn sensory mechanisms. Top-down processing depends on things we have learnt from past experience, such as that saucers are a certain size and likely to stay in the same place; if we receive inputs from a large saucer-shaped flying object, we may 'see' it as a meteorite — or a UFO — depending on our learned expectations.

SAQ 12

On cheques which have to be read by computers there is a separate shape for each letter and figure, each of which could be recognized by an appropriate template.

SAQ 13

'Round' letters like C O D and G would have more features in common with Q and so the decision would have to be made higher up in the system. An 'angular' letter like a T could be distinguished from a Q at the first level of detecting curved or straight lines.

SAQ 14

Gestalt theory (Section 1.3) might support a template model because of its emphasis on whole figures. Hubel and Wiesel's work (Section 1.1) showed that in the brain of the cat nerve cells lower down in the visual system transmit simple information like dots and lines while cells higher up respond only to more complex inputs like angles and corners, thus providing physiological evidence for a Pandemonium-type feature detection model.

SAQ 15

Both template and feature detection models are bottom-up because sensory information is passed upwards for more complex analysis. Taking the context of letters into account would involve top-down processing based on our learned knowledge about word spellings in English.

SAQ 16

An experienced gardener would start with a set of perceptual models (schemas) of all the different types of weeds and flowers. He or she might analyse features of the leaves which indicate that the plant is a marigold. This perceptual model of a marigold would lead the gardener to look at other features like the shape and bushiness of the plant as further confirming cues.

SAQ 17

Neisser's cyclic model means that Neisser as a psychologist has a model (or theory) about how perception works. The perceptual models refer to the mental models that all human beings (including Neisser!) generate in order to recognize sensory inputs as objects.

SAQ 18

The analysis of features involves bottom-up processing; the synthesis of perceptual models based on expectations involves top-down processing. In Neisser's model, perception emerges from an interaction between both sorts of processing.

SAQ 19

A threshold is defined as the level of stimulation which a person can report being aware of 50% of the time. For an input to be definitely subthreshold, it would have to be flashed in the tachistoscope for so brief a time that people could not report seeing it.

SAQ 20

Introspective reports can reveal the products of perceptual processing, i.e. the actual sensations and perceptions we are consciously aware of. However, it is impossible to obtain verbal reports about the unconscious bottom-up and top-down processes which give rise to these perceptions.

SAQ 21

A computer is an example in which information is typed in, various calculations are carried out inside the machine, in order to produce an output. A calculator is another example.

SAQ 22

Perception is also concerned with the registration and recognition of stimulus inputs in the input processes stage.

SAQ 23

Broadbent's model is a bottom-up model because the selective filter operates on the basis of sensory features, like ear of arrival, or other physical characteristics of the stimulus.

SAQ 24

The fact that the subjects in Grey and Wedderburn's experiment found it easier to group the words 'cat', 'ate', 'mouse' together implies that knowledge of word meanings must have been influencing their selective attention in a top-down direction.

SAQ 25

Cherry's findings indicate that people can notice something about both channels at once which goes against Broadbent's single channel theory. However, the fact that subjects only noticed physical characteristics of the unattended message supports the idea that selection occurs on the basis of sensory analysis.

SAQ 26

Broadbent's theory would presumably predict that you wouldn't hear the verbal message about the bomb because you would be attending only to the single (shadowed) channel, although you might hear the fire-bell because a switch to the other ear might be triggered by a physical characteristic like a loud bell. Treisman's model would allow you to attend to either signal because they could both reach the recognition stage in an attenuated form.

SAQ 27

Treisman's model is still a bottom-up model because the selection of input channels into a main channel and attenuated channels occurs at the level of sensory analysis. Recognition of meanings only occurs after this initial selection so attenuated channels have to be really important to force their way through to the recognition stage.

SAQ 28

Instead of one channel being selected for attention, the inputs from all channels progress as far as the recognition stage. Important inputs are then selected to enter conscious awareness, regardless of which input channel they originally arrived on. If an unattended message is recognized (unconsciously) as important, it can be selected for conscious attention. This still leaves the problem of how unconscious recognition occurs.

SAQ 29

In Broadbent's model, items in the unattended channel are completely blocked out, although items from other channels are stored briefly in the sensory buffer and so can be attended to if attention can be switched quickly enough. In Treisman's model, items in the unattended channel are attenuated and will only be attended to if they are important enough to be recognized. In the Deutsch/Norman model, items in all channels are recognized on an equal basis but only the most important are selected for conscious awareness.

SAQ 30

Evaluation of the attentional demands of various tasks involves top-down processing based on experiences with those tasks. However, the allocation of attention has to take into account bottom-up perceptual analysis of what is going on in the environment.

SAQ 31

In Broadbent's single channel model, parallel input of sensory processes is converted by the selective filter into one channel, in which items are dealt with one at a time by a limited capacity serial processor. In Treisman's model, parallel processing of a partial kind occurs up to the semantic recognition stage, although one main channel of input has already been selected for serial processing. In the Deutsch/Norman model, all inputs are fully but unconsciously processed in parallel up to the recognition stage, after which one set of inputs is selected for serial processing. Thus, in each case, conscious attention is assumed to be serial.

SAQ 32

Neisser's cyclic model of perception (Section 1.7) involves a continuous monitoring of sensory inputs under the guidance of mental perceptual models which have to be adapted if necessary to conform with the evidence of our eyes. All this processing is presumably unconscious and going on in parallel until the final perceptual model is consciously perceived. In the same way, the letters in a visual search task are pre-attentively monitored until conscious attention is focused on the located target letter. It would be just as natural to say that the target letter is perceived at that point, since it matches the internalized perceptual model of the target being searched for, e.g. an O.

SAQ 33

(a) is too temporary a change, unless one thinks that sailors can learn to do this as a special skill. (b) is definitely an example of learning, at least we hope so. (c) is an example of maturation, since the genetic heredity of the human species includes the ability to stand upright; however, some experience is also necessary for a child to learn to walk. (d) is probably due to alcohol, which causes a temporary physiological change rather than a learned response.

SAQ 34

You may have thought of blinking our eyelids if something comes too near our eyes, the knee-jerk reflex to a sharp tap, jumping if we are startled, sweating in the heat, removing a hand from a hot surface. All these are unlearned innate reflex responses.

SAQ 35

NS = bell; UCS = puff of air; CS = bell (after the association between bell and puff has been learned); UCR = eye-blink to puff; CR = blink to bell in the absence of puff (after association has been learned).

SAQ 36

The discriminative stimulus is the classroom and teacher; the behaviours emitted include reading and throwing things; the reinforcement is attention from the teacher; the child's throwing behaviour is reinforced and so becomes more frequent.

SAQ 37

The bell was associated with food so that it drew the pigeon's attention to the presence of reinforcement while it was doing its 'bowling' responses; a lighted button might not have been so noticeable so the pigeon might never have 'twigged' the connection between the desired responses and reinforcement.

SAQ 38

(a) and (d) are true of classical conditioning; (b), (c) and (d) are true of operant conditioning.

SAQ 39

Your answer should be:

	presentation	removal
pleasant	(a) increase	(b) decrease
unpleasant	(c) decrease	(d) increase

(a) and (d) are examples of reinforcement: (a) positive reinforcement (presentation of a pleasant stimulus), (d) negative reinforcement (removal of an unpleasant stimulus). (c) and (b) are examples of punishment: (c) presentation of an unpleasant stimulus, (b) removal of a pleasant stimulus.

SAQ 40

The teacher's attention acted as positive reinforcement because it increased the child's paper-throwing responses. If the teacher had ignored the child's bad behaviour, it might have disappeared through extinction. This would have been most effective combined with the use of positive reinforcement for desired behaviours, e.g. if the teacher had praised the child when he was sitting reading quietly.

SAQ 41

Both punishment and extinction decrease the frequency of responses; punishment does this directly by the presentation of an aversive stimulus, extinction indirectly through withdrawal of a reward.

SAQ 42

In Figure 3.6 the pigeon received its third reinforcement (the third dash) after about 1¾ minutes, by which time it had made about 100 pecks (this can be read off the vertical axis as 100 responses).

SAQ 43

(a) Weekly wages are a fixed-interval schedule and should lead to fast responding just before pay day. (b) Piece-work is a fixed-ratio schedule and should result in a high rate of responding. (c) A fruit machine operates on a variable-ratio schedule, only producing reward after a variable number of responses. This schedule results in a tendency to produce lots of responses without any reinforcement, which is presumably what the manufacturer intended!

SAQ 44

The NS would be the written words on the report, the UCS could be a reward or praise given by the parents, which elicits a UCR of 'joy'. This reward would be the primary reinforcer. After the written report has been paired with the primary reinforcer, it would become a CS eliciting a CR of 'joyful feelings', and so act as a secondary reinforcer. The child would now be expected to increase responses likely to achieve a good report. Of course, it would be necessary to explain why parental praise had become a primary reinforcer in the first place, perhaps by being associated with sweets when the child was very young.

SAQ 45

The primary reinforcer was the grape and the secondary reinforcer was the poker chip.

SAQ 46

You may well have been puzzled by this one. A Skinnerian would say that TV is a reinforcer because it can be demonstrated that access to a telly acts as a reward which tends to increase the probability of responses.

SAQ 47

The only evidence for a drive to watch TV is that people find watching TV rewarding and so will make responses in order to be allowed to watch television. The evidence is 'circular' because it uses the behaviour itself as evidence that a drive has been reduced and then uses the drive to explain the behaviour. This does not worry Skinnerians since they define reinforcement as anything which reinforces behaviour. It is more of a problem for someone like Hull who wanted to explain reinforcement in terms of drives based on biological needs. It is unlikely that the human species was genetically programmed with a biological need to watch TV, although we may have an inbuilt boredom drive!

SAQ 48

In Tolman's theory, an animal learns that, say, the stimulus of a lighted button is a sign of another stimulus: food. In Skinner's terms, the pigeon learns that to make a pecking response in the presence of a lighted button will lead to food. The difference is that Tolman emphasized the animal's learning about the situation even in the absence of a response, whereas Skinner believes that increased responding is the only measure of learning.

SAQ 49

(a) In classical conditioning, the stimulus situation is the pairing of the UCS and the NS and the CR is the learned response. The UCS (e.g. food) can be thought of both as an eliciting stimulus and as a 'reinforcer' which is paired with the NS. (b) In operant conditioning, the stimulus situation is the discriminative stimulus (e.g. lighted button) to which the probability of a learned response is increased by reinforcement. (c) Tolman would say that the animal perceives a relationship between the stimulus situation and reinforcement which guides the learning of an appropriate learned response.

SAQ 50

Tolman's theory is a top-down theory because it implies that internal representations of past experiences (cognitive maps) influence behavioural responses.

SAQ 51

(a) is STM. (b) is LTM. (c) uses information in LTM about how to add, multiply, etc. and STM for the storage of particular digits you have to calculate. (d) involves going over the speeches in STM until you have stored them in LTM, although you will probably not remember them for ever. (e) requires you to retrieve a memory from LTM.

SAQ 52

The similarities between the models are that in both cases there is a flow of information from stimulus inputs which is processed at various stages represented by 'boxes'. However, in Figure 4.1, the storage processes 'box' has been split up into LTM and STM. STM accepts input from the input sensory processes (SM) and either outputs it directly (like a telephone number) or passes it through to LTM. It is also possible for STM to retrieve information from LTM to output it. According to this model, all information has to go through STM at some stage.

SAQ 53

The capacity of SM would be estimated at 75% (of an array of twelve letters very briefly exposed). The duration is half to one second.

SAQ 54

The sensory buffer in Broadbent's (1958) theory is equivalent to the registration of sensory information in SM. The selective filter selects one channel, say a cued row of letters, and passes it through to the limited capacity processor. As you can see from comparing Broadbent's model in Figure 2.3 with Figure 4.1, the limited capacity processor is in fact STM.

SAQ 55

After reading out the trigram, Peterson and Peterson gave subjects a number and asked them to count backwards in threes until they had to recall the trigram.

SAQ 56

(a) and (b) are episodes which are likely to be stored for shorter or longer periods in episodic memory. (c) is general knowledge stored in semantic memory. (d) depends on general knowledge in semantic memory about the rules of the game but the actual cards played would be in episodic memory. You can see that episodic memories may be longer term, e.g. early memories, than recently acquired semantic knowledge, e.g. the rules of a new card game.

SAQ 57

Peterson and Peterson used trigram nonsense syllables consisting of three consonants (see Techniques Box V).

SAQ 58

It might be possible that RI is being caused by the interfering effect of the interpolated task of counting backwards in threes but, since digits are not very similar to nonsense syllables, there may not be much interference. It seems more likely that PI is being caused by interference from trigrams learnt in earlier trials; all the trigrams are very similar so one would expect maximum interference. Also relevant is evidence that recalls get worse as trials progress, indicating a build-up of PI.

SAQ 59

It would be expected that people would make less errors at the beginning and end of lists and more in the middle, so the curve would be the opposite of the one for correct recall.

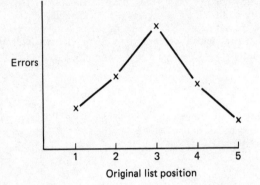

SAQ 60

(a) The number could be remembered as a visual code (the shapes of the numbers), an acoustic code (the sounds of the letters), an action code (the sequences of hand movements needed to dial the number), or a semantic code (recoding the number by reference to your age, car number etc.). (b) The codes would be likely to be a mixture of visual images, motor movements, and semantic coding of verbal instructions. (c) If using a visual code, C, Q and O would be most likely to be confused because they look alike; if using an acoustic code, C, B and T sound alike and so would be more likely to be confused in memory.

SAQ 61

The central executive is responsible for allocating attention to the demands of different tasks and so would be the same as the central allocation of attention in Kahneman's model (see Figure 2.6). Baddeley's central executive suffers from the same problem of who makes the decisions (a little homunculus?).

SAQ 62

Looking out for whether a word like BEAR contains an E should involve 'shallower' processing than deciding whether it is a pleasant word or not, so people would be expected to remember the (b) words better than the (a) words.

SAQ 63

The subjects who had made the 'shallower' physical judgement about whether the words were in upper case or lower case would be likely to do better on a memory test concerning the cases of letters, compared to subjects who had done 'deeper' semantic processing, but may not have even noticed the case of the letters.

SAQ 64

Physical features would be processed by the sensory input processes, phonemic processing of rhyming sounds would take place in STM, while semantic meanings would be coded in LTM.

SAQ 65

Neisser's analysis-by-synthesis model described in Section 1.7 of the Perception Module explicitly refers to Bartlett's use of the term 'schemas' to describe the perceptual models which guide perception.

SAQ 66

Ebbinghaus scores ticks on the 'easy to measure' criterion and examining the precise effects of repetitions and delays on memory for lists of items. Bartlett scores highly for real-life materials and flexibility.

SAQ 67

The independent variable was varying inputs between 'emotional' taboo words and neutral words. The dependent variable was measured by recording how long words had to be exposed in the tachistoscope before people reported that they had recognized what each word was. The predicted relationship was that people would need longer exposure times to report recognizing the taboo words.

SAQ 68

2-7 can be used to measure both human and animal behaviour, although 6 and 7 tend to be used more frequently with animals. 1 is only possible with language-using humans and 9 refers to human patients. 8 is normally confined to animals, except in exceptional cases when human brains have to be investigated for medical reasons, e.g. to avoid harming important functions like speech during brain surgery.

120

References

ALLPORT, D. A. (1980), 'Attention and performance', in Claxton, G. (ed.), *Cognitive Psychology: New Directions*, London, Routledge and Kegan Paul.

ALLPORT, D. A., ATTONIS, G. and REYNOLDS, P. (1972), 'On the division of attention: A disproof of the single channel hypothesis', *Quarterly Journal of Experimental Psychology*, 24, pp. 225-35.

ATKINSON, R. C. and SHIFFRIN, R. M. (1968), 'Human memory: a proposed system and its control processes', in Spence, K. W. and Spence, J. T. (eds), *The Psychology of Learning and Motivation: Advances in Research and Theory*, Vol. 2, New York, Academic Press, pp. 89−195.

BADDELEY, A. D. (1966), 'The influence of acoustic and semantic similarity on long-term memory for word sequences', and 'short-term memory for word sequences as a function of acoustic, semantic and formal similarity', *Quarterly Journal of Psychology*, 18, pp. 302−9, 362−5.

BADDELEY, A. D. (1976), *The Psychology of Memory*, London, Harper and Row. (97)

BADDELEY, A. D. (1981) 'The concept of working memory', *Cognition*, 10, pp. 17−23.

BARBER, P. J. and LEGGE, D. (1976), *Perception and Information*, London, Methuen.

BARBER, P. J. and LEGGE, D. (1985), *Information and Human Performance*, London, Methuen.

BARTLETT, F. C. (1932), *Remembering*, Cambridge, Cambridge University Press (Paperback 1967).

BOLLES, R. C. (1978), *Learning Theory*, New York, Holt, Rinehart and Winston.

BOUSFIELD, W. A. (1953), 'The occurrence of clustering in recall of randomly arranged associates', *Journal of General Psychology*, 49, pp. 229−40.

BOWER, T. G. R. (1977), *The Perceptual World of the Child*, London, Fontana.

BROADBENT, D. (1954), 'The role of auditory localization in attention and memory span', *Journal of Experimental Psychology*, 47, pp. 191−6.

BROADBENT, D. (1958), *Perception and Communication*, Oxford, Pergamon.

BROWN, R., and KULIK, J. (1977), 'Flashbulb memories', *Cognition* 5, pp. 73−79.

BRUNER, J. S. and POSTMAN, L. (1947), 'Emotional selectivity in perception and reaction', *Journal of Personality*, 16, pp. 69−77.

CHERRY, E. C. (1953), 'Some experiments on the recognition of speech with one and two ears', *Journal Acoustical Soc. of America*, 25, pp. 975−9.

COGNITIVE PSYCHOLOGY (D303), Milton Keynes, Open University Press.

COLTHEART, M., LEA, C. D. and THOMPSON, K. (1974), 'In defence of iconic memory', *Quarterly Journal of Experimental Psychology*, 26, pp. 633−41.

CONRAD, R. (1964), 'Acoustic confusion in immediate memory', *British Journal of Psychology*, 55, pp. 75−84.

CRAIK, F. I. M. and LOCKHEART, R. S. (1972), 'Levels of processing: a framework for memory research', *Journal of Verbal Learning and Verbal Behaviour*, Vol. 11, pp. 671–84.

CRAIK, F. I. M. and TULVING, E. (1975), 'Depth of processing and the retention of words in episodic memory', *Journal of Experimental Psychology*, 104, pp. 268–94.

DEUTSCH, J. A. and DEUTSCH, D. (1963), 'Attention: some theoretical considerations', *Psychological Review*, 80, pp. 80–90.

EBBINGHAUS, H. (1885), *Uber das Gedachtnis*, Leipzig, Dunber, H. Ruyer and C. E. Bussenius. Published in translation (1913) as *Memory*, New York Teachers' College Press.

FANTZ, R. L. (1961), 'The origin of form perception', *Scientific American* 204, in Coopersmith, S. (ed.), *Frontiers of Psychological Research*, San Francisco, Freeman.

GARCIA, J. and KOELLING, R. A. (1966), 'Relation of cue to consequence in avoidance learning', *Psychonomic Science* 4, pp. 123–4.

GIBSON, J. J. (1966), *The Senses Considered as Perceptual Systems*, Boston, Houghton-Mifflin.

GIBSON, J. J. (1979), *The Ecological Approach to Perception*, Boston, Houghton-Mifflin.

GRAY, J. A. and WEDDERBURN, A. A. I. (1960), 'Grouping strategies with simultaneous stimuli', *Quarterly Journal of Experimental Psychology*, 12, pp. 180–4.

GREENE, J. and D'OLIVEIRA, M. (1982), *Learning to Use Statistical Tests in Psychology: A Student's Guide*, Milton Keynes, Open University Press.

GREGG, V. (1975), *Human Memory*, London, Methuen.

GREGORY, R. L. (1966), *Eye and Brain*, London, Weidenfeld and Nicolson.

GREGORY, R. L. and WALLACE, J. (1963), *Recovery from Early Blindness*, Cambridge, Heffers.

HARLOW, H. F., HARLOW, M. K. and MEYER, D. R. (1950), 'Learning motivated by a manipulation drive', *Journal of Experimental Psychology*, 40, pp. 228–34.

HUBEL, D. H. and WIESEL, T. N. (1959), 'Receptive fields of single neurons in the cat's striate cortex', *Journal of Physiology*, 148, pp. 574–91.

HULL, C. L. (1943), *Principles of Behaviour*, New York, Appleton-Century Crofts.

INTRODUCTION TO PSYCHOLOGY (DS262), Milton Keynes, Open University Press.

KAHNEMAN, D. (1973), *Attention and Effort*, Englewood Cliffs, N.J., Prentice Hall.

KOHLER, W. (1925) *The Mentality of Apes*, New York, Brace and World.

LEGGE, D. and BARBER, P. J. (1976), *Information and Skill*, London, Methuen.

LINDSAY, P. H. and NORMAN, D. A. (1972), *Human Information Processing*, London, Academic Press.

MANDLER, G. (1967), 'Organisation and memory', in Spence, K. W. and Spence, J. T. (eds), *The Psychology of Learning and Motivation*, Vol. 1, New York, Academic Press, pp. 327–72.

MCKAY, D. G. (1973), 'Aspects of the theory of comprehension, memory and attention', *Quarterly Journal of Experimental Psychology*, 25, pp. 22–40.

MILLER, G. A. (1956), 'The magical number seven, plus or minus two: some limits on our capacity to process information', *Psychological Review*, 63, pp. 81–97.

MILLER, G. A. (1972), *Psychology: The Science of Mental Life*, Harmondsworth, Penguin.

MILLER, G. A., GALANTER, E. and PRIBRAM, K. H. (1960), *Plans and the Structure of Behaviour*, New York, Holt, Rinehart and Winston.

MORRIS, C. C., BRANSFORD, J. D. and FRANKS, J. J. (1977), 'Levels of processing versus transfer appropriate processing', *Journal of Learning and Verbal Behaviour*, 16, pp. 519–33.

MURDOCK, B. B. Jnr. (1962), 'The serial position effect in free recall', *Journal of Experimental Psychology*, 58, pp. 193–8.

NEISSER, U. (1963), 'Decision-time without reaction-time: experiments in visual scanning', *American Journal of Psychology*, 76, pp. 376–85.

NEISSER, U. (1967), *Cognitive Psychology*, New York, Appleton-Century Crofts.

NEISSER, U. (1976), *Cognition and Reality*, San Francisco, Freeman.

NEISSER, U. (1982), *Everyday Memory Observed: Remembering in Natural Contexts*, San Francisco, Freeman.

NEISSER, U., NORICK, R. and LAZAR, R. (1963), 'Searching for ten targets simultaneously', *Perceptual and Motor Skills*, 64, pp. 644–65.

NORMAN, D. A. (1968), 'Towards a theory of memory and attention', *Psychological Review*, 75, pp. 522–36.

NORMAN, D. A. (1976), *Memory and Attention* (2nd Ed.), Chichester, Wiley.

OPEN UNIVERSITY DS262, *Introduction to Psychology*, Milton Keynes, Open University Press.

OPEN UNIVERSITY D303, *Cognitive Psychology*, Milton Keynes, Open University Press.

PAVLOV, J. P. (1927), *Conditioned Reflexes*, Oxford, Oxford University Press.

PETERSON, L. R. and PETERSON, M. J. (1959), 'Short-term retention of individual items', *Journal of Experimental Psychology*, 58, pp. 193–98.

SEGALL, M., CAMPBELL, D. T. and HERSKOVITZ, M. J. (1966), *The Influence of Culture on Visual Perception*, New York, Bobbs-Merrill.

SELFRIDGE, O. G. (1959), 'Pandemonium: a paradigm for learning' in *Mechanization of Thought Processes*, HMSO, London.

SELIGMAN, M. E. P. (1971), 'Phobias and preparedness', *Behavioural Therapy*, 2, pp. 307–20.

SHAFFER, L. H. (1975), 'Multiple attention in continuous verbal tasks', in Rabbitt, P. M. A. and Dornic, S. (eds), *Attention and Performance V*, London, Academic Press.

SKINNER, B. F. (1938), *The Behaviour of Organisms*, New York, Appleton-Century-Crofts.

SKINNER, B. F. (1953), *Science and Human Behaviour*, New York, Macmillan.

SKINNER, B. F. (1974), *About Behaviourism*, London, Jonathan Cape.

SPERLING, G. (1960), 'The information available in brief visual presentation', *Psychological Monograph 74*, No. 498.

THORNDIKE, E. G. (1932), 'Reward and punishment in animal learning', *Comparative Psychology Monographs*, 8 (whole No.39).

TOLMAN, E. C. (1932), *Purposive Behaviour in Animals and Men*, New York, Appleton-Century-Crofts.

TOLMAN, E. C. and HONZIK, C. H. (1930), 'Introduction and removal of reward and maze performance in rats', *University of California Publications in Psychology*, 4, pp. 257–75.

TREISMAN, A. (1960), 'Contextual cues in selective listening', *Quarterly Journal of Experimental Psychology*, 12, pp. 242–8.

TREISMAN, A. (1964), 'Verbal cues, language and meaning in selective attention', *American Journal of Psychology*, 77, pp. 206–19.

TULVING, E. (1972), 'Episodic and semantic memory', in Tulving, E. and Donaldson, W. (eds), *Organisation of Memory*, New York, Academic Press, pp. 381–403.

VON BEKESY, G. (1957), 'The ear', *Scientific American*, in Coopersmith, S., *Frontiers of Psychological Research*, San Francisco, Freeman.

WALKER, S. (1984), *Learning Theory and Behaviour Modification*, London, Methuen.

WATSON, J. B. (1924), *Behaviourism*, Chicago, University of Chicago Press.

WOLFE, J. B. (1936), 'Effectiveness of token-rewards for chimpanzees', *Comparative Psychology*, Monograph 12, No. 60.

Names Index

Pavlov, I. P. (1927) 49
Peterson, L. R. and Peterson, M. J. (1959) 79

Segall, M., Campbell, D. T. and Herskovitz, M. J. (1966) 10
Selfridge, O. G. (1959) 18
Seligman, M. E. P. (1971) 57
Shaffer, L. H. (1975) 38, 41
Skinner, B. F. (1938) 51
Skinner, B. F. (1953) 51
Skinner, B. F. (1974) 51
Sperling, G. (1960) 75

Thorndike, E. G. (1932) 51
Tolman, E. C. (1932) 66
Tolman, E. C. and Honzik, C. H. (1930) 67
Treisman, A. (1960) 31
Treisman, A. (1964) 31
Tulving, E. (1972) 80

Von Bekesy, G. (1957) 4

Walker, S. (1984) 70
Watson, J. B. (1924) 46
Wolfe, J. B. (1936) 64

Index of Concepts

128